THE CURSE OF THE

MUMMY

THE CURSE OF THE
MUMMY

UNCOVERING
TUTANKHAMUN'S TOMB

CANDACE FLEMING

SCHOLASTIC
FOCUS
NEW YORK

Library of Congress Cataloging-in-Publication Data

Names: Fleming, Candace, author.
Title: The curse of the mummy : uncovering Tutankhamun's tomb / Candace Fleming.
Other titles: Uncovering Tutankhamun's tomb
Description: First edition. | New York : Scholastic Focus, an imprint of Scholastic Inc., 2021. | Includes bibliographical references and index. | Audience: Ages 8–12. | Audience: Grades 4–6. | Summary: "During the reign of the New Kingdom of Egypt, the boy pharaoh Tutankhamun ruled and died tragically young. In order to send him on his way into the afterlife, his tomb was filled with every treasure he would need after death. And then, it was lost to time, buried in the sands of the Valley of the Kings. His tomb was also said to be cursed. Centuries later, as Egypt-mania gripped Europe, two Brits—a rich earl with a habit for gamblin... ...'or years to redisc... ...and once Tutankhamun's tomb... ...covered, would a... ...looting the ph... ...rious illn... ...d?"

Identi... 60000487153 ...ack) |

Subjects: ... ...erature. |
Carter ... George
Edwa ... venile
lit ... he
Kings— ... ature. |
Va... NW ... e. |
Egypt—H ... literature.

Classification: LCC DT87.5 .F54 2021 | DDC 932/.014—dc23
LC record available at https://lccn.loc.gov/2020056427

1 2021

Printed in the U.S.A.   23
First edition, September 2021
Book design by Abby Dening

ACKNOWLEDGMENTS

I have a wonderful friend and editor in Lisa Sandell. I can't thank her enough for her exacting standards, unflagging encouragement, and distinctive vision. The curse! Who would have thought? Thanks, also, to the talented team at Scholastic who make me look so good. I am deeply indebted to Dr. J. J. Shirley, Managing Editor of the *Journal of Egyptian History* and Director of the Theban Tomb 110 Epigraphy & Research Field School, for sharing her time, knowledge, and passion for ancient Egypt by reading the manuscript for accuracy. Her comments and insights were priceless . . . as was her son's book review. Finally, and as always, my love and gratitude to Eric Rohmann for being a fine travel companion, an excellent mapmaker, and a pretty great research assistant.

ACKNOWLEDGMENTS

THE CURSE OF THE
MUMMY

TABLE OF CONTENTS

A NOTE TO READERS

I have used the spelling of the boy king that is most favored by Egyptologists. It should be noted that the spellings of ancient Egyptian names are based on the translation of hieroglyphs, which can be changed into English in various ways. This means there are many different spellings of ancient names, and especially of Tutankhamun... Tutankhamen ... Tutankhamon.

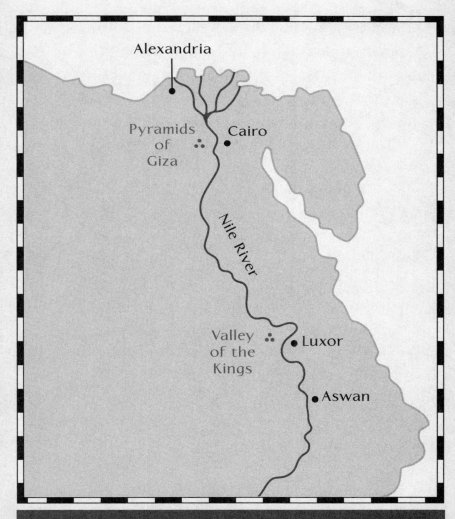

Alexandria

Pyramids
of
Giza

Cairo

Nile River

Valley
of the
Kings

Luxor

Aswan

A map of Egypt.

It was said . . . the boy king's tomb was cursed.

In an underground burial chamber, in the flickering shadows made by their oil lamps, high priests had carried out ancient, mysterious rituals. As specified by *The Book of the Dead*, they had summoned protective demons and placed charms in the tomb's walls. They had recited spells and prayers.

And, said some, they had conjured up a terrible curse.

Some claimed the curse had been carved above the tomb's entrance and read:

DEATH WILL SLAY WITH ITS WINGS
WHOEVER DISTURBS THE PEACE OF THE PHARAOH.

Others argued it had been inscribed on the lid of the stone sarcophagus:

O ANYONE WHO ENTERS THIS TOMB, WHO WILL
MAKE EVIL AGAINST THIS TOMB:

MAY THE CROCODILE BE AGAINST HIM ON WATER,
AND THE SNAKE AGAINST HIM ON LAND.

MAY THE HIPPOPOTAMUS BE AGAINST HIM ON
WATER, AND THE SCORPION AGAINST HIM
ON LAND.

Still others insisted it had been etched onto a magic brick and hidden beneath a chest containing the pharaoh's internal organs:

IT IS I WHO DRIVES BACK ROBBERS FROM THE TOMB
WITH FLAMES OF THE DESERT.

I AM THE PROTECTOR OF TUTANKHAMUN'S GRAVE,
AND I WILL KILL ALL THOSE WHO CROSS THIS
THRESHOLD . . .

But all agreed the curse existed. And it had but one purpose: *deadly protection.*

Who would be foolish enough to deny the curse?

Who would be foolish enough to defy it?

CHAPTER 1

Sands of the Past

1324 BCE–1906 CE

On a spring night, more than thirty-three hundred years ago, a silver-bright moon cast a ghostly radiance on the cliff and crags of Egypt's Theban foothills. Down a remote desert path came a handful of men. Shovels in hand and sticking to the shadows, they walked silently as cats. Soon they reached the floor of the Valley of the Kings.

A dark figure wearing the uniform of a royal necropolis guard stepped into the moonlight. What had he been promised in return for revealing the burial spot? A precious jar of scented oil? A gold bracelet? Wordlessly, he led the men along the Valley floor.

For the past five centuries, Egypt's pharaohs had been buried in this remote valley. Bounded on all sides by towering cliffs and hills of rocky debris, it seemed the ideal resting place for their mummies and their treasures. This was crucial. Egyptians believed a tomb was an important symbol of continuity, of eternity, of a ruler passing from the living world to that of the gods. For this reason, it was important that a dead king's body not be disturbed after it had been laid to rest.

Originally, the pharaohs had built huge pyramids as their resting places. But not even these structures' fake doors and secret chambers could keep the kings' remains safe. The showy structures quickly attracted robbers, who broke in, stealing gold and tearing the sacred mummies apart. And so Egypt's rulers, in search of a safer place to be buried, had chosen this valley. They began cutting secret tombs deep into the rock and covering their entrances with rubble and sand. So cleverly hidden were these tombs that they were almost impossible to find.

Even the guard didn't know where most of the pharaohs were buried. But he *did* know the location of one tomb, that of the recently interred King Tutankhamun.

Tutankhamun had ascended to the throne around the age of eight. Too young to rule alone, he'd been guided by powerful advisers with their own plans and policies. They made the decisions, but he got the credit. An inscribed sandstone slab at Karnak Temple in Thebes (modern-day

Luxor) told of the boy king's great accomplishments: "Now when his majesty arose as king, the temples and estates of the gods and goddesses, from Elphantine to the marshes of the Delta had fallen into ruin . . . Their shrines had fallen down and turned into ruin . . . The land was in confusion and the gods had turned their backs on the land . . . Hearts were faint in bodies because everything had been destroyed." But Tutankhamun had stepped forward to rebuild the temples and sanctuaries. He'd offered nourishing foods to the deities. "The [Egyptians] all rejoice and celebrate . . . because good has come back into existence." They praised Tutankhamun for restoring the traditional religion of the land, something his predecessor had tried to change. They saw the boy king's word as law, and his acts as inspired by the gods. And then, when he was just eighteen years old, Tutankhamun unexpectedly died. The ancient funerary rites immediately kicked in.

The pharaoh's corpse was taken from his place of death (the name of which has been lost to history) to a temple on the west bank of the Nile. Here, priests washed the body in natron, a natural dehydrating agent. Next, the embalmers shaved the body and removed the king's brain with an iron hook through the nose. They poured resin into the skull through the nose cavity and made an incision on the left side of the body. This incision allowed an embalmer to remove the king's stomach, intestines, lungs, and liver. These were embalmed separately and placed in four stone jars, a different one for each organ. Only the heart stayed in the body. It was believed the heart was the "seat of the mind," and that the god Osiris would judge it against a *ma'at* feather, the symbol of truth and rightness.

Once emptied, priests stuffed the body cavity with more packets of natron. They placed even more packets around it. Then they left the body to dry out for thirty to forty days. When they finally returned, they rubbed oil into the now desiccated body, filled it with packing materials, and applied several layers of expensive perfumed ointment. This took another thirty-five days.

At last, they began encasing Tutankhamun's body in bandages. Each limb was wrapped separately. Golden covers were slipped over fingers and toes. A pair of golden sandals were placed on the feet. As the entire body disappeared beneath lengths of fine linen, the priests recited prayers and placed dozens of amulets and jewelry, as well as two ceremonial daggers, between the layers. Finally, they fitted a golden mask on the head over a linen sheet to which they stitched golden hands holding the crook and flail, symbols of the pharaoh's authority. Four golden bands inscribed with spells meant to help the king's soul in the afterlife tied everything into place.

About seventy days after Tutankhamun's death, his funeral procession had made its way from the chapel on the bank of the Nile to Tutankhamun's underground tomb in what would become known as the Valley of the Kings.

Had the guard watched the procession pass?

Along the way, priests had chanted. Mourners had wailed. And twelve servants in white tunics had strained

Tutankhamun's funeral procession as depicted on the east wall of his burial chamber.

at the ropes as they pulled the sledge bearing the king's mummy across the hot sand. Behind the mummy came hundreds more servants. They struggled beneath the weight of the king's possessions—chests of clothes and jewelry, weapons and chariots, thrones and beds and chairs, baskets of food and flowers, vessels of oil and wine—*everything* he would need in the afterlife.

When the burial party reached the tomb's entrance, the mummy was propped upright facing the sun so various rituals could be performed. Traditionally, the king's eldest son, who was to succeed his throne, should have carried these out. But Tutankhamun didn't have a son. And so Ay, a high-ranking official who claimed the throne for himself, stepped forward to perform one of the key parts of the funeral rites, the Opening of the Mouth. Using what Egyptians believed was a magical adze, Ay touched the mummy's face mask. This, it was believed, allowed the dead king to breathe, walk, and talk in the afterlife.

Then Ay and the other mourners left the Valley. But the priests remained. They reverently placed the king's mummy in its final resting place and arranged his treasures in the four rooms of his tomb. They uttered spells and prayers. Finally, they left, pressing the seals of the pharaoh as well as the Royal Necropolis into the door's wet

One of the three scenes painted on the north wall of Tutankhamun's burial chamber, this depicts the boy king's heir, the elderly Ay, performing the all-important "Opening of the Mouth" ceremony.

plaster. Then they climbed the rock-cut stairs back into the sunlight. Under their watchful eyes, necropolis workers hid the staircase with sand and rock. Then, sweeping up behind them so their footprints would not disturb the harmony of the tomb, the priests left.

Tutankhamun, they believed, was safely on his way to the afterlife.

But the guard, like so many other necropolis workers, knew the location of this fresh burial site. And this knowledge was worth money.

Now he stopped and pointed. The small depression in the rubble was barely noticeable unless someone was looking for it.

The robbers were looking for it.

Quickly, they dug away sand and gravel, uncovering the rock-cut stairs. Not daring to light a torch, they descended

A photograph showing a hole made by robbers in order to enter the tomb of Tutankhamun.

into the darkness until they came to a door blocked with stone and plastered over. It took but a moment to make a hole and shimmy through. Still in darkness, feeling their way along a narrow passage, they came to a second door. The robbers shimmied through this one, too. They found themselves in a chamber. Blackness pressed in on them. The silence felt close and thick. At last, one of the thieves lit a reed torch with cord and spindle. Shadows suddenly danced over the glittering heaps of treasure. Before them stood a wooden statue of a god with hands upraised as if in horror at finding them there. Entering a pharaoh's tomb was a violation of sacred beliefs. Weren't the thieves terrified of the king's mummy that lay nearby? Did they fear the wrath of ancient gods? Did they worry about a curse?

Obviously not. The thieves scattered, their footsteps echoing as they moved through the tomb's chambers. Upending chests and rummaging through boxes, they searched for small items of gold and silver, jewelry and beads, jars of perfumes and pots of cosmetics. Easy to carry, these small objects were also easy to sell.

There wasn't much time. Too soon the sun would come up, and with it, the necropolis priests. The men did not

Found near the tomb entrance, a twisted linen scarf into which one of the robbers had wrapped eight gold rings. The robber either dropped his loot on the way out or tossed it back into the chamber because he feared being caught in the act.

want to get caught. The punishment for robbing a royal tomb was death.

At last, bags full, the sweaty, dirt-streaked robbers rushed back through the passageway and up the stairs into the cool of the starry desert night. Drinking in the fresh air, they disappeared into the shadows.

These two images show the damage done to tomb artifacts as robbers rifled through them in search of portable treasure. The numbers seen in the top photo were placed there thousands of years later by excavators.

*   *   *

With the rising sun came the discovery of the break-in. Necropolis priests tidied up the tomb's disheveled rooms. They stuffed clothing and jewelry back into boxes. They righted chairs. Finally, they repaired the blocked and plastered doors. As an extra precaution, they filled the passageway from floor to ceiling with tons of white limestone chips. Once more, they concealed the tomb's entrance with sand and rock.

But the thieves returned. Again, they cleared the staircase and made a hole in the first blocked and plastered door. The now stone-clogged passageway did not stop them. Tunneling over the stones at the top left, they again entered the tomb. They shook out cabinets and overturned chests. Again, they took smaller, lighter objects. Again, they disappeared into the night.

The next morning, necropolis priests discovered this second break-in. Using the same tunnel the robbers had made through the limestone chips, the priests entered the tomb yet again. This time they didn't bother to tidy up all the mess left by the ransacking thieves. Instead, they simply checked to make sure the mummy was intact. Then they filled in the robbers' tunnel with yet more limestone chips and sealed the doors. They buried the staircase and concealed the tomb entrance.

This pattern of robbery and restoration would have repeated itself over and over. Tutankhamun's tomb, like most others in the Valley, would have been plucked clean. But then something unusual happened.

It rained.

And rained.

And rained.

The rushing water cut out wide furrows and pushed along sand, stone, and boulders. The Valley turned into a churning, muddy lake. And when the storm ended and the floodwaters drained away, not a sign of Tutankhamun's tomb remained. It had vanished beneath a thick layer of mud, shale, and limestone.

The vanished tomb, like the king buried inside, was soon forgotten. Even later tomb builders did not know it existed. Digging out other burial places for other pharaohs, the builders piled their trash on top of the entrance to the now long-forgotten tomb. As the centuries passed, so much dirt and rock was piled up there that it looked like nothing but a mountain of debris. So worthless did later tomb builders consider the spot that they even erected workmen

The entrance to the Valley of the Kings with El-Qurn, a pyramid-shaped mountain, towering in its background.

huts on top of it. They never knew that beneath it all, in utter darkness and total silence, lay the boy king, Tutankhamun.

Untouched.

Forgotten.

Century after century after century.

Time, like the Nile River, flowed.

Ancient Egypt, once so powerful, gave way to rulers from other lands. The old beliefs disappeared. No more mummified pharaohs were buried in treasure-filled tombs. No more prayers were whispered in the great

The Great Sphinx, pictured in this eighteenth-century watercolor, buried up to its neck in sand.

Thousands of years of blowing sands cover the great temples, as shown in this eighteenth-century drawing.

temples. Desert sand drifted over the Sphinx. It buried monuments and palaces and temples, while the names of the once-great rulers were scattered to the wind. So were the ancient chants and spells. So many thousands of years passed that people remembered next to nothing about the

The Egyptians thought nothing of living among the ancient ruins, as this nineteenth-century photograph of a woman carrying water through the rubble of Karnak Temple in Luxor shows.

world's longest-lasting civilization. Even the ancient written language of hieroglyphs was lost, vanished like those tombs and temples, buried in the sands of history.

Those who came after the ancient Egyptians—the Nubians, Assyrians, Persians, Romans, the Muslim Caliphates, Mamluks, Ottomans—repeatedly stumbled across artifacts. New rulers re-inscribed monuments to themselves, or dismantled them to build new temples. They chiseled off inscriptions from crumbling walls. Mummy cases were broken up for firewood, and corpses were ground into a powder that many believed could cure broken bones and stomachaches.

And so it went for thousands of years, until 1798, when French general Napoléon Bonaparte and his army arrived in Egypt. Although Bonaparte's purpose for being there was military (he hoped to seize the route to India from Great Britain), he also brought along a team of scientists and artists to study Egypt. He believed they could help him understand, and ultimately conquer, the country. Six years later, when the French left, they took with them crates of priceless antiquities. They didn't ask permission to remove these artifacts. Who would they have asked? The Ottomans had lost control of Egypt after being defeated by Napoléon's troops. In turn, British forces had

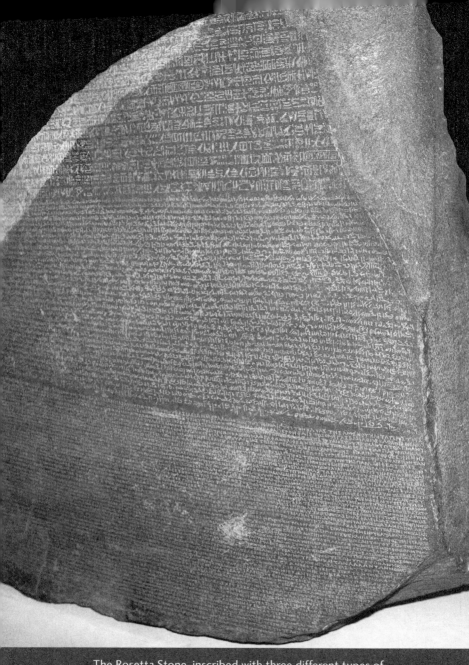

The Rosetta Stone, inscribed with three different types of script, is still in the British Museum today.

defeated the French. And so the scientists hurried back to Paris with stolen amulets, figurines, and scarabs. They also took monuments that required the help of hundreds of soldiers to move—sarcophagi, obelisks, an enormous ram's head, and a colossal fist of Pharaoh Ramesses II. The prize of this entire collection was a stone found near the town of Rosetta. With its three versions of a royal decree—the first in hieroglyphic text; the second in Demonic, a kind of shorthand version of hieroglyphic text; and the third in Greek—it unlocked the mystery of the ancient Egyptians' long-forgotten language. But the scientists didn't get to keep the Rosetta Stone. The British seized it, along with some of the larger artifacts, for their own museum collection in London.

Once back in Europe, the French scientific team published a series of books titled *Description of Egypt*. Its luminous illustrations and fairy-tale descriptions of ancient Egypt's riches caused a sensation. Egyptian mania gripped Europe. People scrambled to collect all things Egyptian. Museum directors and diplomats, nobles, wealthy businessmen, and everyday tourists descended on Egypt in search of gold necklaces, alabaster jars, scarabs, mummies, *anything* they could lay their hands on. Some visited Egypt's ancient sites themselves with pickaxes and shovels. Others bought their treasures from so-called antiquities dealers.

Some of these dealers, like the Italian treasure hunter Giovanni Belzoni, scoured the desert, rediscovering and excavating forgotten monuments and temples. Was his purpose scientific? Hardly. Claiming the property as his own, he emptied tombs and carted away entire monuments. He sold them to the highest bidder. Much of his loot ended up in private collections. One such artifact,

This 1816 watercolor painted by Giovanni Belzoni shows his workmen taking a huge granite head of King Ramesses II from the mortuary temple in Luxor where it had resided for thousands of years. Belzoni sold the head to the British Museum, where it can be found today.

the alabaster sarcophagus of Seti I, ended up in the basement of a wealthy London architect named John Soane. It remains there today.

Other antiquities dealers sold merchandise they'd bought from tomb robbers. As more and more people clamored for Egyptian antiquities, prices skyrocketed. It quickly became clear to villagers living in and around the Valley of the Kings that the contents of the nearby tombs were far more valuable than they'd ever imagined. Why shouldn't they reap the fruits of the earth—*their* earth— and seize what was just lying there for the taking? Giving up farming, many villagers joined the already-frantic digging. But in the search for more beautiful and extraordinary finds, tourists, locals, and tomb raiders alike trampled and destroyed thousands of smaller artifacts. Few bothered to excavate systematically. Few were concerned about a scientific approach. After all, they were seeking treasure, not knowledge. And there was always something to be found . . . sold . . . collected.

"At every step . . . the excavator is aware of the be-jeweled and mummified dead just below the surface waiting to be discovered," one enthusiastic treasure hunter wrote in her diary. "Whether you go up the great river [Nile], or strike off . . . across the desert, your horizon

A 1905 photograph of British tourists being assisted by local men on their climb up the Great Pyramid at Giza. Trampling on archaeological sites was neither forbidden nor frowned upon in those days.

is bounded by mounds, or ruins, or by ranges of mountains honey-combed with tombs."

And so, Egypt's treasures were looted and scattered all over the world, with some of the most beautiful and archaeologically important antiquities being stored or displayed thousands of miles from their Nile homes.

There *was* an Antiquities Service, created in 1858 to stop ancient treasures from being looted and sold. But Frenchmen rather than Egyptians ran it. Since the days of Napoléon's expedition, the French had ruled the roost in all matters concerning Egypt's antiquities. Everything else in Egypt—its defense, police, foreign affairs, finances, and public works—would (by the 1880s) effectively be controlled by the British. But both countries, in a rare moment of compromise, agreed that a Frenchman would always fill the post of director of the Antiquities Service.

It was the second director, a portly, middle-aged French Egyptologist named Gaston Maspero, who recognized that the Antiquities Service needed money—lots of it. Money not only to excavate, but also to preserve what had already been uncovered. To guard temples and tombs, to restore them and record the inscriptions covering their walls before time and tourists destroyed them. But how could all this be accomplished when the Service received almost no public funds?

Maspero began cultivating foreign archaeological teams from museums and universities, as well as European and American millionaires. His idea was to give them a "concession," or license to dig. They would assume the cost and the risk of excavation, but their work would be under the control and supervision of the Antiquities Service. In this way, excavation could continue without costing Maspero's department a cent. Better yet, the Service got half of anything the digger found, as well as all royal mummies, coffins, and sarcophagi, and any artworks of archaeological importance. These would go to the brand-new museum in Cairo.

There *was* one exception to the fifty-fifty division of found treasure: an intact royal burial. If a pharaoh's or queen's tomb had gone undisturbed since ancient times, then *all* the artifacts—every single one—would go to the Egyptian museum.

Diggers happily agreed to these rules, including the last restriction. After all, up to this time, no one had found a tomb that hadn't been plundered thousands of years earlier. And plundered tombs, they were learning, could still be full of astonishing objects that early robbers had considered worthless—paintings, statuettes, delicate alabaster vases.

Then, too, there were surprises. Hadn't one digger uncovered a commonplace crocodile mummy only for its case to crack open and reveal a priceless papyrus roll? And what about the mummified hand of an unknown woman found in an underground tomb? It had been covered with exquisite and priceless golden bracelets. There was no telling what might be found next. Private collectors, antiquities dealers, wealthy businessmen, European aristocrats, and representatives from some of the world's greatest museums shared the feeling that anything was possible.

"The exploration is a kind of chase," explained one digger. "You think you have discovered a scent. You follow it. You lose it and you find it again. You go through every phase of . . . excitement, hope, disappointment, exultation."

Was it any wonder, then, that a rich and good-natured British earl with a knack for gambling (and winning) decided to try his luck at digging in Egypt?

CHAPTER 2

The "City of the Dead"
DECEMBER 1906

George Edward Stanhope Molyneux Herbert, Fifth Earl of Carnarvon—or "Porchy" to his friends—looked out across his excavation site near the Valley of the Kings. A hundred workers raised clouds of hot dust as they shifted, dug, and moved rubble by the basketful. Beneath the flap of canvas that had been built to provide him a scrap of shade, Carnarvon mopped his face with a silk handkerchief. And to think this was the *cool* time of year. That's why all excavation seasons began in late fall and ended in early spring. It was just too hot to dig otherwise. Not for the first time, he wondered about the sensibleness of digging in a three-piece tweed suit. Of course, *he* never picked up a shovel. Lord Carnarvon was more of a director, pointing out first one spot and then another to his workmen.

The debonair Lord Carnarvon, seen here resting on a shaded veranda. He never completely healed from his car accident in 1901.

It was a haphazard approach. Why, wondered many people, hadn't the earl, with all his money, hired an archaeologist to help him? It was obvious the British aristocrat knew next to nothing about excavation.

What locals didn't know was that Carnarvon was getting advice from beyond the grave. Or so he believed. Ever since his arrival in the Valley four weeks earlier, he'd been receiving a steady stream of cables from Velma, his London-based psychic. Velma claimed the ancient priests of Egypt themselves had been whispering messages for Carnarvon into his ear. Velma, in turn, had passed along these ghostly communications. But so far—even with this ghostly advice and after four very hot, very dull weeks— the earl hadn't found a single treasure.

Then, too, his excavation site was a dud. Little more than a mound of rubble, it sat in a corner of the Theban necropolis, or "city of the dead." Thousands of years earlier, the necropolis had been filled with graves and mortuary temples where the living had gone to pray and leave sacrifices for the dead. Untold riches had once lain beneath the sand and rock. But ancient tomb raiders, as well as modern-day treasure hunters and tourists, had turned the site into a confusing jumble of debris. From the towering piles of dirt left by previous diggers protruded thousands of potsherds, shreds of mummy wrappings, fragments of coffins, and trash. To uncover any object would have required moving tons of rubble, something Carnarvon didn't understand. Still, he remained optimistic. Every time the workers' shovels dug into a new patch of sand, he felt a rush of adrenaline.

To Carnarvon, digging was a lot like gambling. And

the earl knew plenty about that subject. He loved playing cards and placing bets on horses. He'd once loved racing down country roads in fast cars, too. But just a few years earlier, he'd had an automobile accident. His injuries had been severe—temporary blindness, a crushed chest, burned legs, and dislocated arms. From that day on, Carnarvon was never completely well again. His lungs were especially weak, so his doctor had suggested he begin wintering in a drier climate. Carnarvon had chosen Egypt. Its tombs and temples captivated him. At first, he threw himself into buying artifacts at markets and from dealers. But he soon decided buying them wasn't enough. He wanted to dig. Luckily for him, he was one of the richest and most connected men in England. A few words from the earl to government officials had landed him permission to dig. Carnarvon threw himself into his new sport.

Digging here.

Digging there.

A well-dressed Englishman on donkey-back now appeared at Carnarvon's site. Dismounting, the man tossed the reins to one of the workers and turned to the earl.

A smile must have twitched under Carnarvon's mustache. Here was Arthur Weigall, an inspector who worked

Arthur Weigall (far right on donkey-back) riding into the Valley.

for the Antiquities Service. He'd come to check up on the excavation.

The men shook hands, and Weigall asked if the earl had found anything.

Carnarvon pointed to a basketful of mummy fragments and broken bones. That was it. Nothing beautiful or rare. Nothing important.

Weigall had expected this. It was he, after all, who'd palmed off this worthless site on the earl. He'd done it on purpose. A trained archaeologist, Weigall detested the idea of letting rich treasure hunters dig around willy-nilly. "The records of the past are not ours to play with," he repeatedly said. It wouldn't have been quite so bad if Carnarvon had hired an archaeologist. To dig successfully, one needed knowledge as well as money. It was Weigall's hope that after coming up empty-handed, Carnarvon would return to England and never come back.

Moments later, the workmen shouted and then fell silent. They rested on their shovels and looked into the pit they'd dug. Carnarvon's *reis*, his foreman, beckoned excitedly for the Englishmen to come.

Carnarvon slapped his wide-brimmed hat onto his head and hurried out into the sun. Weigall followed. Moments later, they peered down at a partly exposed black object. Weigall asked for a hand brush. But it was Carnarvon who knelt down and gently cleared the dirt from the find. With each brushstroke, more and more of the object was revealed.

Yellow eyes.

Bristling whiskers.

It was the wooden coffin of a mummified cat.

Working together, Carnarvon and Weigall lifted the small coffin from its millennia-old grave. Sitting in the sun at the edge of the pit, it looked—with its sinister glowing eyes—wild and dangerous.

Weigall estimated it was three thousand years old.

A mummified cat similar to the one Lord Carnarvon found.

"My first important find!" whooped Carnarvon.

Hardly. Mummified cats were common. Thousands had been found in tombs and ancient sites all up and down the Nile. But Weigall didn't tell him this.

Cradling his find, Carnarvon headed for his waiting

donkey. He was eager to get back to his hotel in Luxor and show his wife, Lady Almina.

"I wonder what I will find next?" he exclaimed as he climbed onto the donkey's back.

It looked as if Weigall's plan to get rid of the earl had backfired. Finding the mummified cat had only made him keener to dig. Hopes dashed, the inspector mounted his own donkey and followed Carnarvon into town.

It was said . . . the cat took its revenge.

As Arthur Weigall later recalled in his essay "The Malevolence of Ancient Egyptian Spirits," he arrived home late on the night of Carnarvon's find. As he made his way in darkness to his bed, he tripped over the cat coffin. Confound it! Why had his Egyptian servant left the artifact on the bedroom floor? Sent over from the hotel hours earlier, it should have been put away in the storage shed until its shipment to the museum in Cairo. So why was it here?

Annoyed, Weigall rang the bell for help.

No one came.

Weigall rang again.

Still no one responded.

Where the devil was everyone?

The inspector stomped down the hall and into the kitchen.

Chaos!

The servant crouched in a corner, swatting at the air and screaming while the rest of the staff huddled around him.

"A gray cat! A gray cat!" cried the servant.

Weigall demanded to know what was happening.

The servant had been stung by a scorpion, explained one of the staff. Delirious from the insect's poison, he claimed a large gray cat was chasing him.

"A gray cat!" cried the servant.

Obviously, the coffin would not be removed until morning. Leaving the delirious servant in the others' care, Weigall went back to his room.

Moonlight shone through his open windows and fell on the black figure of the cat coffin. Stepping around it, the inspector climbed into bed. But he found it impossible to sleep. Instead, he stared at the coffin. Its eyes seemed to glitter malevolently.

Down the hallway echoed the cries of the servant: "Keep the cat away from me! Keep the cat away from me!"

At the sound of the cries, the cat's eyes seemed to glow even brighter. A shadow passed over its face, and Weigall shuddered. Had the thing just turned its head to look at him? He could have sworn it had. A strange thought sprang into his mind. The cat was angry for being disturbed. The archaeologist was sure of it. They'd dug it up. They'd had no right.

There came a loud noise—BANG!—like a firecracker.

Weigall sat upright . . . just as a gray cat hopped onto the bed. Dashing across the inspector's knees, it leaped out the open window and into the moonlit garden beyond.

A cold fear spread through Weigall's veins. Slowly, he turned to look at the cat's coffin. It had fallen open, its two halves still rocking on the floor. Between them sat the mummified cat. Its bandages, Weigall claimed, had been ripped open around the neck as if the spirit of the dead feline had burst out of them.

Questions raced through Weigall's mind. Had the coffin fallen open simply because of its age? Was the gray cat just a night wanderer? Or was something more sinister at work? Something supernatural? Perhaps the cat's spirit, furious at having its burial site disturbed, had decided to wreak havoc on the living.

But that was impossible. Wasn't it?

Another thought struck him.

If a *cat* could do all this, imagine what the spirit of an angry pharaoh might do.

CHAPTER 3

Enter Howard Carter

DECEMBER 1908

Seated at his desk in the Cairo museum, Gaston Maspero, director of the Egyptian Antiquities Service, peered over his wire-rimmed glasses at the British aristocrat sitting before him. So, Lord Carnarvon wanted an archaeologist to help him dig, eh? As Carnarvon had explained it, the discovery of the cat mummy had indeed whetted his appetite for more discoveries. And so, with the ancient spirits still guiding him, he'd haphazardly dug for yet another season . . . and still had found nothing but odds and ends. To find something wonderful, Carnarvon finally admitted, he needed a *living* expert. Could Maspero recommend someone?

Only one name came to the director's mind: Howard Carter. "He is a friend of mine," said Maspero. "A very knowledgeable man. I'm sure you'll find him helpful." The

director paused. Should
he tell the earl about the
trouble Carter had gotten
into? He decided against
it. Instead, he added simply, "But let me warn
you, my lord, [he] is an
extremely stubborn man."

Carnarvon was not
put off. "A stubborn man
is a determined one, after
all," he replied. He wanted

Gaston Maspero, Director of
the Egyptian Antiquities Service
from 1881–1886 and again from
1899–1914.

to meet this Howard Carter as soon as possible.

As he did most mornings, Howard Carter hiked up the
steep slope to the eastern edge of the Theban Mountains.
The air was oven hot and the soft sand underfoot made
climbing difficult. But he didn't slow his pace. Short,
stocky, and strong, he knew the terrain well. For more
than fifteen years, the Egyptian desert had been his home.
He'd explored its barren valleys and jagged mountain
peaks. He'd crawled through its hidden tunnels and slept
in its forgotten tombs. But *this* was his favorite place. The
view from the cliff top never failed to take his breath away.

In the distance, he could see the blue ribbon of the Nile River threading its way from south to north. Bordering it on both sides ran a bright green strip a mile or two wide. These fields of sugarcane and sesame seed, corn, wheat, and okra grew in the rich black silt left behind by the river. But the green abruptly changed to the tans and browns of the desert sand that stretched into the horizon. The desert sand reached all the way up the ridge to where Carter stood, too.

His dark eyes scanned the line between the cultivated land and the barren desert. Ancient Egyptians had

The line between the living and the dead can be seen in this modern-day aerial photograph, which captures the lush green along the Nile River giving way to barren desert.

believed this was the boundary between the world of the living and the world of the dead. It was here, where the two met, that many vast temples had been built. Carter's gaze rested on a collection of ruined columns and two giant weathered statues—all that remained of those once-magnificent structures.

Carter turned back the way he'd come, then stood for a moment looking out at the ridge. Nestled behind it, below a pyramid-shaped mountain peak called El-Qurn, waited the Valley of the Kings. Just the name thrilled Carter. It conjured up images of secret tombs, priceless treasure, and royal mummies.

Other archaeologists believed that little remained to be found in the Valley. But Carter felt certain a royal tomb was still out there. Hidden. Untouched. Its treasures intact. And he was convinced it belonged to the one king for whom neither a mummy nor an empty tomb had ever been found . . . Tutankhamun.

But Carter despaired of ever getting the chance to search for the tomb—or *any* tomb, for that matter. For the past two years, he'd lived hand to mouth, without a job, and completely ignored by the wealthy Westerners who paid for archaeological digs. His career appeared to be over.

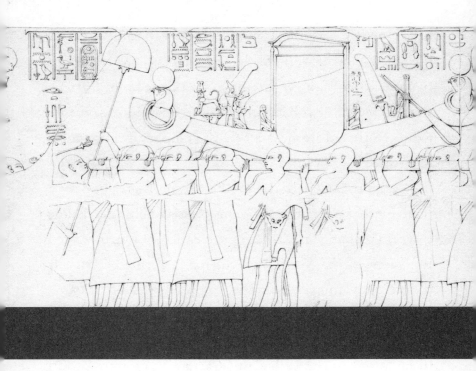

But not so long ago, he'd been a rising archaeological star.

Howard Carter arrived in Egypt from England in 1891. Just seventeen years old at the time, he had little schooling, no money, and no training in Egyptology. He *did*, however, have a knack for sketching and painting. His father, Samuel, had taught him. An artist, Samuel scraped out a living by working on England's country estates, painting portraits of the aristocracy's beloved horses and hounds.

This pen-and-ink drawing done by Howard Carter around 1916 of a relief in Luxor Temple shows his skill in re-creating ancient Egyptian art.

Young Carter went with him. He would have preferred going to school, but his father couldn't afford it. Instead, the boy had to start making a living as soon as possible. "I have nothing to say about my education . . . nature thrusts some of us into the world miserably incomplete," he wrote with some bitterness years later. By the age of fifteen, he began getting small jobs of his own: "drawing . . . portraits of pet parrots, cats and snappy, smelly lap dogs."

One estate where Carter found regular work was Didlington Hall. Its owner, Lord Amherst, was an avid collector of ancient Egyptian artifacts. In his garden loomed seven massive black statues of Sekhmet, the lion-headed goddess who tore men to pieces at the request of the sun. In his library lay the fragments of a papyrus scroll covered with flowing script. And in the great hall sat brightly painted coffins and golden statues, blue scarabs made of faience—a type of glazed ceramic ware—beaded necklaces, amulets, and more. When not painting dogs and horses, Carter filled his sketchbook with gods and goddesses, mummies and coffins. He developed a feeling for Egyptian art—he was "hooked." He longed to go to Egypt.

And that's when luck stepped in. During a visit to the hall, a British Egyptologist named Percy Newberry noticed Carter's sketches. It just so happened that Newberry was looking for "a non-gentleman artist" who would work for cheap. In those days, working-class people like Carter were not considered equals by the rich and well educated. In the eyes of Newberry, the teenaged artist was *not* a gentleman. And so, because he was "miserably incomplete," Carter got his first break. The seventeen-year-old headed to Egypt.

He traveled by steamship to the port city of Alexandria, and by train to bustling Cairo, by ferry across the Nile River, and by donkey up a steep desert trail to a set of tombs carved high in the cliffs to the excavation camp.

Howard Carter had arrived at his new life.

That first night as he lay on a rough mattress made of woven palm sticks, he felt exhausted, overwhelmed, and a little homesick. But he also felt exhilarated. He was, he told himself, "on the eve of an adventure."

For months afterward, from early morning to late at night, he copied the paintings that decorated the long, winding tunnels of the dark tombs. In those days before color photography, Egyptologists desperately needed someone who could reproduce the hues and details of Egyptian art. But Carter was more than a copyist. He sketched rocks and cliffs. He sketched the desert wild-life, especially the birds—buzzards, ravens, and blue rock pigeons.

And luck smiled on Carter again. Flinders Petrie, the man who invented the idea of archaeology as a science and today is known as "the father of archaeology," noticed the boy's keen eye. He asked Carter to join his excavation team. Soon, the teenager was sketching by day and study-ing by night. From Petrie, he learned . . . *everything*! How to deal with ancient, fragile textiles; how to date a pot based on its style; how to move boulders; how to read the gorges and sand dunes; how to keep tunnels from collaps-ing; how to keep from being eaten alive by the sand fleas.

Most importantly, Petrie taught him the study of "unconsidered trifles." At that time, most diggers cared only about big finds—tomb paintings, sculptures, or jewelry. But Petrie advocated something new: "the observation of small things . . . The science of observation, of registration, of recording." Nothing escaped Petrie's eye. Unlike other Egyptologists, he took note of a single bead or amulet, corroded coins, and other fragments of the ancient Egyptian's everyday life. He sifted through sand. He sifted through rubble. He collected every shard of pottery, then pieced them together like a huge jigsaw puzzle. And while some Egyptologists laughed at his methods, Carter listened and learned. Within two years, and under Petrie's close eye, he himself was searching for clues in the sand.

Nineteen-year-old Carter's days now passed in the daily grind of excavation. Under a burning sun, he worked alongside his crew—twenty-two Egyptian men in white galabiya robes—sometimes shoveling for hours. The instant something was found, work stopped. Then Carter jumped into the pit to decide what to do next. Delicate objects often needed on-the-spot conservation so they wouldn't turn to dust at first touch. Larger pieces had to be carefully hauled out. With every artifact he found, he drew conclusions about how ancient Egyptians lived. He imagined and speculated about them. He "played" with the objects he found, and "perplexed" himself with the many questions and possibilities they presented.

In his spare time, Carter taught himself to read hieroglyphs. He studied ancient history. And he became fluent in Arabic—something most other Westerners didn't bother with—so he could get to know the Egyptian workers.

What he didn't do was make friends with the excavation crowd. Despite his talents, he knew the others didn't consider him an equal. He was still an outsider. He understood that to make good in archaeology, he would need stubbornness and an iron determination. He would also need a firm belief in himself.

For the next six years, Carter dug in the desert sand and camped under the stars. Then, in January 1901, he caught the attention of Gaston Maspero, Director of the Antiquities Service. Maspero put the rising young archaeologist in charge of the monuments of Upper Egypt—a five-hundred-mile stretch of archaeological sites that included the Valley of the Kings. Many of these sites were open to tourists. In his new job, the twenty-six-year-old kept them safe and in good repair. He also supervised the excavators who held licenses to dig in the area. Were they sticking to the agreement they'd made with the Antiquities Service? Had they found anything worth reporting? At the same time, Carter continued his own digging. And he made some important finds, including the already-robbed tombs of the Eighteenth Dynasty rulers Queen Hatshepsut and King Thutmose IV. So good was Carter at the job that four years later, Maspero decided to make him chief inspector of Lower Egypt. It was a big promotion. Carter would now be responsible for the Great Pyramids near Cairo.

But Carter didn't last long in this job. Just weeks after his transfer, a group of drunken French tourists forced their way into a site after attacking the Egyptian guards. Carter told the guards to fight back. The result was a rowdy brawl that left men on both sides with black eyes and bloody noses.

The incident caused a minor diplomatic storm. "The indignity of letting an [Egyptian] resist a Frenchman weighed more than the indignity of being drunk and disorderly," remarked one British archaeologist. Indeed, the entire European community in Egypt was both insulted and scandalized. How dare Carter allow such a thing? It was tantamount to letting a servant slap his master! And the British very definitely considered themselves Egypt's master. "The Egyptians must do as they are told," declared

Lord Cromer, Britain's head official in Egypt. "They must be kept in check."

Not surprisingly, many Egyptians bristled at doing as they were told. Enraged at being forced to follow British rules, and longing to govern themselves, they demanded an end to foreign interference. "Egypt for the Egyptians!" they cried. Again and again, protests erupted in the streets.

It was British policy to respond swiftly and harshly to these protests. No act of rebellion, no matter how small, could be allowed to go unpunished. How else could Britain hold on to its control? In one instance, after a handful of Egyptian villagers pelted a group of British soldiers with rocks, authorities rushed in. They arrested fifty-two of the villagers. In court, the judges—three British officers who didn't speak Arabic—passed severe sentences on them. Four of the rock-throwing villagers got the death penalty, two went to jail for life, and the remaining received forty lashes of the whip. The hangings and the floggings were carried out the next day. As a warning, the rest of the villagers were made to watch. *This* was why the incident with Carter and the guards could not be ignored. If Egyptians were allowed to beat up the French today, so the thinking went, tomorrow it would be the British.

There was another reason, too. Many Englishmen, as well as other Westerners, believed in the innate superiority of the "white man" and his right to rule over everyone else. It was common for Westerners to use words like "dirty" and "dishonest" when describing Egyptians. They rarely mingled with them socially. And they made no effort to understand their point of view, their culture, their religion, or their language. "It is ridiculous to apply western democratic notions to a people so brutish, so insensitive, so mentally deficient as the Egyptians," noted one British woman who spent a winter season in Cairo. They had no choice, reasoned Westerners, but to protect and rule these ignorant, inferior people. It was the British justification for controlling Egypt, and it pervaded almost all interactions with Egyptians.

Carter, too, was influenced by these prejudices. He thought himself fair and reasonable, and compared to others of his generation, he was. He spoke Arabic. He visited the homes of his Egyptian acquaintances and ate meals with them. In truth, he felt easier with them than with those "gentleman" archaeologists. But he behaved condescendingly toward the Egyptians and believed he was a superior Briton.

Still, when higher-ups in the Antiquities Service

demanded Carter apologize to the French tourists, he refused. *He* hadn't done anything wrong, he insisted, and neither had the guards. And when Howard Carter believed he was right about something, he never, ever backed down. Instead of apologizing, he quit.

His colleagues expected him to return to England. Instead, Carter went to Luxor. For the next two years, he scratched out a living painting pictures of ancient ruins for tourists. He worked for tips as a tour guide. He was even seen in Luxor's bazaars, offering his expertise to Europeans looking to buy antiquities. For a fee, he steered them away from fakes (of which there were many) and helped them bargain for real treasures. But he did not work as an archaeologist. Despite his vast knowledge, no one would hire him. Carter had taken the Egyptians' side over his fellow Europeans', and most could not forgive him for that. Every single Egyptologist in the country blacklisted him . . . except Maspero.

When Carter came down off the slope that December morning in 1908, a message from the director of antiquities awaited him. An opportunity had come across the official's desk. A job. Was Carter still licking his wounds over that unfortunate event with the French tourists?

Maspero certainly hoped not. Here was a chance for Carter to get back in the archaeological game.

Carter hesitated. He'd have to meet this Lord Carnarvon first. After all, he didn't want to work for someone unwilling to dig scientifically. Still . . . maybe his luck was changing.

Two days later, Carter stepped into the lobby of the Winter Palace. Luxor's finest hotel, it boasted marble salons, crystal chandeliers, and a white-gloved, well-trained staff who anticipated their guests' every whim. Only the wealthiest visitors stayed at the Winter Palace. Naturally, Lord Carnarvon resided here. He'd taken the best suite—one with a wide balcony overlooking the Nile. It was here the two men met.

Carnarvon invited his guest to take a seat. Staring across the table, they took stock of each other. That afternoon, the intense, brooding, and work-roughened Carter would learn that Carnarvon, despite being inexperienced in most things archaeological, was determined and enthusiastic. And the aristocratic, fashionably dressed Carnarvon would discover that Carter lived for just one thing—to make a great find. Both recognized how well they complemented each other. With Carnarvon's money

The Winter Palace, Lord Carnarvon's home away from home whenever he was digging around Luxor.

and Carter's knowledge, they were sure to uncover incredible things.

They also discovered they shared a dream: to dig in the Valley of the Kings. But for now they could only stand by and watch as American millionaire Theodore Davis made discovery after discovery. According to the Antiquities Service rules, the excavation process was organized by concession, meaning only one person at a time could dig in a specific area. Until Davis decided to give up his concession and leave the Valley, Carter and Carnarvon would have to dig elsewhere.

But where?

Carter unrolled the map he'd brought along. All business, he pointed out possible sites. For the time being, they would have to settle for digging near the Valley. Perhaps in the cliffs above Hatshepsut's temple? Or the bottom of the slopes of Dra Abu el-Naga?

But Carnarvon wasn't ready to talk about the nitty-gritty of excavating yet. Instead, he called over a waiter. He insisted they raise a glass to their new partnership.

Would it be successful?

They'd have to wait and see.

A 1908 photograph of Queen Hatshepsut's temple at Deir el-Bahri. The partners would dig around this site for several seasons, finding, among other things, beads and amulets, an ox skull, and a coffin containing the female mummy of a woman named Maartu, as well as the walls and foundations of an unfinished temple meant for Hatshepsut.

It was said . . . a mummy's curse haunted London's British Museum.

The curse emanated from artifact #22542: the coffin lid of a priestess of Amen-Ra. According to newspaper accounts, anyone who gazed upon the object felt its unseen force. Recalled one museum visitor, "As I looked into the painted face of the Priestess on the outside of the lid, her eyes seemed to come to life, and I saw a look of hate in them that turned my blood to ice."

How had the museum come to own such a malevolent object?

A sensational magazine article published in 1909, and quickly reprinted by newspapers around the world, told the tale:

It began with five English friends who traveled down the Nile to the Valley of the Kings. There a treasure hunter approached them. He showed them the lid, recently stolen from its tomb. The friends bought it, then drew straws to see which of them would get to keep it. Arthur F. Wheeler won. He thought himself lucky. But just three days later, one of his traveling companions, Thomas Douglas Murray, had an accident while hunting near the pyramids. His gun exploded for no reason, blowing off his left hand. Weeks later, while returning to England with the lid, Wheeler received a telegram telling him that two of his servants had unexpectedly died. Back in London, Wheeler gave the lid to his fiancée. But she soon came down with a mysterious ailment. Then her mother suddenly died, and her pets went insane.

Wheeler, now terrified of the lid, packed it up and left it in a London warehouse. Soon afterward, he lost his entire fortune in a card game. Moving to America, he borrowed some money and bought a farm. But he suffered floods and a fire. He never recovered financially.

Meanwhile, his sister, Mrs. Warwick Hunt, removed the lid from the warehouse and displayed it in her parlor. When her friend, a psychic named Madame Helena Blavatsky, saw the lid, she exclaimed, "It radiates evil!" But Mrs. Hunt didn't heed the warning. Instead, she invited a photographer to take a picture of the lid. He did . . . and died two days later. That's when Thomas Douglas Murray, the man who'd lost his hand in the gun accident, insisted Mrs. Hunt get rid of the cursed lid. She agreed. She gave it to the British Museum.

Arriving there in 1889, it was placed on display. Mrs. Hunt felt relieved. The curse, she believed, had been vanquished. "The priestess had only used her powers against those who brought her into the light of day and kept her as an ornament in a private room," she said. Now the ancient spirit could rest in peace.

Or could it? Newspaper reporters began asking questions.

If the priestess was at peace, why did museum workers refuse to go near the lid?

Why did a society girl pitch headlong down the museum's stairs after taunting the priestess "to do her worst"?

Why had a well-known artist been trampled by a horse on Great Russell Street after sketching the lid?

Why did some visitors claim they could feel the priestess's ghost standing beside them?

Why did one museumgoer claim that after looking at the lid, he was tormented for weeks with visions of ancient Egyptians peeping at him from behind curtains and over balconies?

Why indeed? wondered thousands of newspaper

readers. Many took the story as proof that the Egyptians had possessed the mystical secrets of the universe. The spirits of Egypt's dead still roamed the earth. Ancient artifacts doled out misfortune. And mummy curses *did* exist.

Didn't they?

═ CHAPTER 4 ═

Ten Seasons Beneath the Theban Sun

1909–1919

On their first morning as partners, in January 1909, Carter and Carnarvon looked out over their concession—a well-searched spot in the Theban necropolis near the old village mosque.

"I think we should dig there and there," said Carnarvon, pointing with his silver-handled walking stick.

"No," replied Carter. "We select one area, then clear it to the bedrock systematically with a long-term plan in mind. There's only one way to discover tombs, and that's by clearing away the rubble and examining the bedrock for signs of disturbance." That rubble, he added, would have to be sifted three times so as not to miss even the tiniest objects.

If Carnarvon was surprised by Carter's lack of deference to him—an aristocratic gentleman—he didn't show it. Instead, he listened closely as the archaeologist went on about systematic and scientific methods. Already, on this first day, there was no doubt that Carter was in charge.

And there was no doubt that Carnarvon had much to learn.

"I'll pitch my tent over here," the earl said sometime later that day. Carnarvon, of course, wouldn't be sleeping overnight in it. He planned on returning each night to his luxurious rooms at the Winter Palace.

Again, Carter said no. The spot the earl had chosen was too far away from the workmen. If anything was found, one or both of them needed to be right there. Unsupervised workmen often pocketed discovered objects. And why wouldn't they? They were poor men with families to feed. That's why, in addition to their daily pay, workers would be rewarded for anything they found. Hadn't Carnarvon done this before? It was, Carter explained, standard procedure at *professional* excavations.

Carnarvon chose to ignore his new partner's arrogance, too.

And so their adventure began.

Nearly three hundred men and boys labored to clear the rock and sand. Their wages alone came to almost five thousand pounds sterling (almost $500,000 in modern US dollars), plus additional expenses for tools and equipment, and feed for the pack animals. Carnarvon didn't do anything cheaply. He liked his pleasures, and unlike some excavators who simply ate sardines from a tin can along with their men, the earl dined aristocratically even in the desert. All his personal food came from Fortnum & Mason, an exclusive grocer in London. In the shade of his tent with the sand swirling around him, he sat down

A *reis* (far left) oversees workers at one of Carnarvon and Carter's earlier excavations. Winding lines of men carry sand and rock from the excavation site in baskets, some precariously balanced on heads and shoulders.

at a linen-covered table to dine on minced beef tongue, curried fowl, biscuits, and pickles, among other delicacies.

Carnarvon's insistence on luxury, as well as his belief in spirits and séances, irritated Carter. But he mostly ignored what he called the earl's "tommyrot." He knew Carnarvon was deeply committed to their excavations. The earl listened carefully to Carter's long-term plans and bowed to his knowledge. He asked questions, sometimes so many that Carter turned gruff. One visitor to their dig recalled that Carter sometimes "spoke to [the earl] as if he were a naughty child."

Carnarvon chose to ignore his partner's snappishness, too.

Excavation work, after all, was backbreaking, painstaking, and dangerous. Up before dawn, Carter worked all day alongside his men, digging, sifting, often finding nothing but sand. He lowered himself by rope into suffocating dark holes, swaying precariously from side to side as he descended. He crawled through tight, unstable tunnels filled with bats and bad air. Time and again, he returned to the surface covered with grime, gasping for fresh air, and . . . empty-handed.

His job didn't end at night. As the sun sank, he checked on the health and well-being of his workers. Did any

Workmen digging a trench. In the background can be seen one of the hand-propelled cars that rumbled over miles of railroad track installed by Carnarvon and Carter to move bigger loads of spoil to a spot far from the excavation site.

scrapes or cuts need bandaging? Was everyone drinking enough water? Afterward, he photographed the day's finds and conserved fragile objects. And he spent hours writing down every detail of the day's work. Nothing was left unrecorded. He'd learned from Petrie that even the most seemingly trivial items could be important later. Once all that was done, he tackled the bookkeeping. Carnarvon expected an accounting of expenses, and Carter kept close track of every penny spent. By the time he closed his eyes, it was often close to midnight.

He found tombs. That first season, they cleared the burial chamber of Tetiky, a mayor of Thebes (ca. 1525 BCE), recovering lots of pottery and a poorly preserved mummy. The next several seasons, they worked on the gusty cliffs of Dra Abu el-Naga. It was hard work. The wind kept refilling the trenches as quickly as the men dug them. Still, they found a rock-cut tomb with eighteen entrances. Built for mass burials, the tomb held sixty-four coffins, some furniture, and a gorgeous silver-bronze statue of a boy. "I shall never forget the sight," wrote a thrilled Carnarvon. "There these coffins had remained untouched and forgotten for two thousand years."

None of these were extraordinary finds. The area they worked was too picked over by previous diggers for that.

Still, it was the most sustained and serious digging Carter had ever done. In this time, he perfected his fieldwork techniques and record-keeping skills. He was developing into a top-notch archaeologist. If he ever found an intact royal tomb, he'd be ready.

Carter had also developed a deep respect for the man who not only paid the bills but also acted as a sounding board. As their years together passed, the two men became friends and confidants. They could, they felt, talk with each other about anything. So close did they become that when Carter decided to build a house near the entrance to the Valley of the Kings, Carnarvon gifted him with all the red bricks for its construction.

Both men still brooded over the Valley of the Kings. Carter especially was sour about not having the chance to dig there. Since teaming up with Carnarvon, he'd been studying and thinking, poring over ancient documents and records, carefully noting previous excavators' finds. "If I had not been an archaeologist, I would have been a detective," Carter liked to say.

And he was hot on the trail of that lost pharaoh, Tutankhamun. More than ever, he believed the king's tomb was there in the Valley. He'd even formed a theory explaining why it hadn't been found. Carter believed one

VALLEY OF THE KINGS

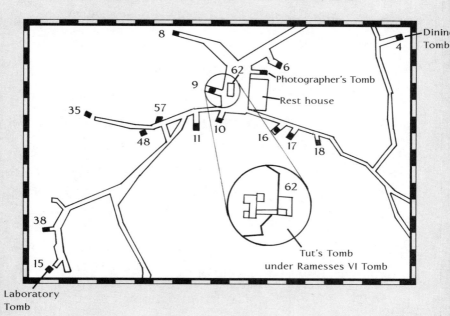

8 Merenptah

Dining Tomb
4

62
6 Ramesses IX

Photographer's Tomb

9 Rest house

35

57

48

10

11

16

17

18

62

Tut's Tomb
under Ramesses VI Tomb

38

15

Laboratory
Tomb

TOMBS

4 Ramesses XI	11 Ramesses III	35 Amenhotep II
6 Ramesses IX	15 Seti II	38 Thutmose I
8 Merenptah	16 Ramesses I	48 Amenemopet
9 Ramesses VI	17 Seti I	57 Horemheb
10 Amenmesse	18 Ramesses X	62 Tutankhamun

A map of the Valley of the Kings. Currently, there are sixty-five known tombs in the Valley, some of which have been open since antiquity. Beginning in 1827, each tomb has been labeled with the abbreviation KV, which stands for King's Valley. The labeling starts with KV 1 (the tomb of Ramesses VII) and so far goes up to KV 65 (an as-yet-unexcavated tomb discovered in 2019). Tutankhamun's tomb is KV 62.

of the Valley's rare downpours had erased the tomb, first from sight and then from memory. It hadn't already been found because . . . well . . . Carter thought Theodore Davis an arrogant, careless treasure hunter who knew next to nothing about systematic methods.

Carter, on the other hand, had a theory based on archaeological evidence.

He explained it to Carnarvon one day.

Unrolling his map of the Valley, Carter pointed to a triangle he'd drawn on it. He explained that inside the area of the triangle, Davis had found objects that Carter believed pointed to the existence of Tutankhamun's tomb. There had been a green faience cup discovered behind a boulder and marked with the pharaoh's name. Later, Davis's team had found forty crude pottery jars in an unmarked pit. These had been filled with clay cups, animal bones, and some wreaths made from leaves and flowers, and one of them had been covered with a linen cloth inscribed with the name "Tutankhamun." Davis believed the jars were little more than ancient trash. But Carter theorized they were the leftovers from the boy king's funeral feast. And then there was the strip of thick gold foil discovered in a crude little chamber dug into the side of a gully. The foil was engraved with a picture of Tutankhamun riding in a

A clue to the boy king's whereabouts, this green faience cup found behind a boulder in the Valley and marked with Tutankhamun's cartouche, helped convince Carter that the king's tomb had yet to be discovered.

chariot. Davis claimed it as proof that the puny chamber was actually Tutankhamun's tomb. But Carter believed Davis was wrong again. That little hole wasn't a pharaoh's tomb. No, it was another clue pointing to the fact that Tutankhamun's tomb was somewhere inside his triangle.

Carter ached to explore this area.

Instead, he kept sifting through mounds of uninteresting rubble.

And Davis kept digging in the Valley.

Until, at last, in the spring of 1914, Theodore Davis gave up his concession. "The Valley of the Kings is now exhausted," he declared.

Egyptologists agreed. Even Gaston Maspero believed there was nothing more to find.

But Carnarvon seized the concession. It had taken fourteen years, but finally, *finally* the Valley was his.

And then?

World War I broke out in Europe, and almost all excavations in Egypt shut down. Lord Carnarvon returned to England. Too old to fight, but eager to do his part for the war effort, he turned his country estate, Highclere, into a military hospital.

Carter remained in Egypt. It was his home now. He settled into his simple brick house, nicknamed "Castle

Carter," just a twenty-minute donkey ride from the Valley of the Kings.

Since he spoke fluent Arabic and had an excellent knowledge of Egypt's terrain, he worked for the British foreign office in Cairo. Rumor had it that he also worked as a spy for the British government. But if he did, his activities remain top secret even today. Mostly, though, Carter spent the war simply filling time. He copied reliefs in Luxor Temple and scoured the antique markets, picking

"Castle Carter" with its oasis-like lawn and trees against the backdrop of the Valley of the Kings.

up bargains in the depressed wartime market and selling them to such institutions as the Cleveland Museum of Art and the Metropolitan Museum of Art in New York City. He grabbed a few bargains for Lord Carnarvon, too. He was, he admitted, "sometimes depressed and sometimes happy." Life in Egypt without sifting through mounds of rubble or hearing the sounds of singing workers was lonely. At times, he felt "nearly dotty."

By 1917, the war began to wind down, and archaeological activity slowly restarted in Egypt. Although Carnarvon remained in England, the partners wanted to do something. Carter examined his map of the Valley, the one with the triangle drawn on it. Where in that area should they excavate first? Carter chose a small spot close to the tomb of Ramesses VI.

It was not a promising start. After eight weeks, all he had to show for his work was a handful of dusty pottery pieces. Still, Carter was hopeful. Certainly, they would find something next season.

Another year passed, and in November 1918, the war officially ended. But all the upheaval in its aftermath made a full season of work in the Valley impossible. Still, Carter couldn't let the desert's cool winter months go by without getting his hands a little dirty. And so, for a single week in February 1919, he and a dozen men cleared a tiny area in front of Thutmose I's tomb. Carter thought of this effort as tidying up rather than excavating. Again, he found nothing.

Four months later, he boarded a ship to England. It would be nice to escape Egypt's burning summer months. It would be even nicer to see Lord Carnarvon again.

It was said . . . Lord Carnarvon spoke to the dead.

On a summer's night in 1919, darkness shrouded Highclere Castle's upstairs guest bedroom. Not a glimmer of moonlight penetrated the thick curtains that had been pulled across the windows. The only light came from a single candle flickering on the mantel. Shadows, eerie and otherworldly, danced across the velvet-flocked walls. They danced, too, across the faces of the four people who sat holding one another's hands at a round table.

Suddenly, a bowl of flowers in the table's center began to rise, slowly, all by itself. The people's eyes widened in horror and astonishment as it floated above their heads. For long moments, it seemed suspended on air. Around the table there were gasps. It was impossible!

The spell suddenly broke. As if released by ghostly hands, the flower bowl dropped back onto the table with a thud. Startled, the spectators dropped hands. Then one of them, Lord Carnarvon, laughed.

This wasn't the first time he'd seen objects levitate. For

years, he'd been hiring clairvoyants and holding séances at his estate. He also employed palmists to read his palm, and fortune-tellers to glean his future from the depths of their crystal balls.

There wasn't anything unusual about this. Spiritualism, a fashionable craze at the time, was practiced all over Europe, as well as the United States. Aristocrats and commoners alike were sitting around in circles, holding hands and hoping to make contact with the dead. Even Queen Victoria of England had held regular séances in her palaces. As for Lord Carnarvon, his belief in the occult had only deepened since his time in Egypt. All those spells and incantations! The Egyptians' obsession with death and the afterlife had rubbed off on the earl. Was there but a thin veil between the living and the dead? Lord Carnarvon ached to find out.

At the table, another person didn't believe any of it. Levitating flowers and table rappings? Tommyrot! That's what Howard Carter called spiritualism. He was too science-minded to believe in ghost stories. But he wasn't about to argue with his friend and patron. And so, since his arrival at Highclere, the archaeologist had hunted, ridden, dined, and . . . attended séances.

Carter looked across the table to where Carnarvon's

adult son, Porchester, sat. Even in the gloom he could tell the young man felt nervous. Could it be that Porchester—recently home from the war—was thinking about the spirits of dead soldiers?

The fourth person at the table, the psychic medium, Lady Helen Cunliffe-Owen, appeared perfectly relaxed. Reaching up, she straightened the diamond brooch glittering at her throat. At that moment, her face convulsed. Her eyes rolled back and she turned white as a corpse. Her lips worked spastically, trying desperately to form words. Then, in a guttural voice not her own, she spoke.

But what was she saying?

The words were in a language neither Carnarvon nor his son recognized.

But Carter did. "It is Coptic," he said.

Strangely, no one bothered to write down Lady Cunliffe-Owen's garbles. Could they even understand them? Coptic was a type of language descended from the ancient Egyptians. And while Carter knew a few words, he wasn't fluent.

Lady Cunliffe-Owen snapped out of her trance. Her gaze straightened. Her color returned. She even continued with the conversation she'd been having. She didn't remember speaking in a strange language. She seemed completely unruffled by it all.

But Carnarvon was shaken. Had the lady been possessed by an ancient Egyptian spirit? If so, what was it trying to tell him? Had it been a warning from the underworld?

Carter, too, was shaken, but for an entirely different reason. Imagine people believing such tommyrot! Lady Cunliffe-Owen was a fake.

Wasn't she?

CHAPTER 5

A Bird of Gold That Will Bring Good Luck

OCTOBER 1920–NOVEMBER 1922

For the next three years and at Lord Carnarvon's expense, hundreds of men using picks, hoes, and their bare hands moved thousands of tons of rubble. When they first began, the Valley had looked like a quarry, covered in mountains of rock—some as tall as thirty feet—left behind by previous excavators. Carter had been forced to clear those massive waste dumps before he could start on his own hunt. Only then could his men dig through the unexcavated layer of floor debris to the bedrock below. All the while, the sun beat down mercilessly. Sand coated lips and stung eyes. In one spot, poisonous cobras hissed with every shovelful of earth moved. And what had all that time and backbreaking work gotten them?

An unnamed boy poses beside the cache of alabaster jars found in 1920 by Carter in the Valley of the Kings.

Thirteen alabaster jars.

That was it.

Thirteen alabaster jars.

But not a single sign of Tutankhamun's tomb.

It was time, Carnarvon decided, to make some changes. In the summer of 1922, he invited Carter to Highclere Castle.

Lord Carnarvon stood as his butler showed Carter into the library. The earl dreaded this conversation. He knew that what he had to say would make his partner unhappy. But it had to be done. Carnarvon was tired of digging with so little reward. As a horse-racing man, he liked to gamble, but only if the odds were in his favor. And when it came to the Valley, the odds seemed completely stacked against him. It was time to cut his losses.

Carter, however, had guessed the subject of their talk. He'd come with a plan he hoped Carnarvon would approve.

The men shook hands, then settled into chairs near the big stone fireplace. The English countryside could be damp and chilly even in June. Susie, Carnarvon's favorite terrier, curled up on the hearth.

Carnarvon began. He deeply appreciated Carter's years of effort, he said, but he could no longer pay for what had turned out to be a useless endeavor.

Hold on, argued Carter, there was still one more royal tomb in the Valley. He just knew it.

Pulling out his well-worn map, the one with the triangle drawn on it, he pointed. Just below the entrance to the tomb of Ramesses VI, there remained one last small area. They had to search it. Yes, that meant tearing down the crude stone huts that had been built on the spot by ancient tomb workers. But only then would the partners' work in the Valley be absolutely done. Only then would they know for sure.

Carnarvon tried to get a word in.

Carter stands beside a birdcage in the marketplace in Cairo around 1923. Was this where he bought his pet? Some sources say yes. Others say he brought the canary all the way from London.

But Carter plunged on. He would pay for the season himself, he said. Wouldn't Carnarvon hang on to his Valley concession just a little longer? Just for one last season? If he found nothing, he would agree to end their partnership. But if he made a discovery, "It shall belong to [you] exactly as under [our] longstanding agreement," he said.

Carnarvon couldn't resist. What a gamble! It was like the final roll of the dice. He would agree to that . . . and pay for it! One last season.

On October 22, Carter returned to the Valley. With him came a canary in a gilded cage. He hoped its sweet song might soothe his raw nerves.

One last season.

It had to be now . . . or never.

When he arrived at Castle Carter, his foreman, Reis Ahmed Gerigar, and a handful of workmen greeted him.

Should he tell them they had one last season?

Reis Gerigar pointed to the cage. "It's a bird of gold that will bring luck," he said. "This year we will find . . . a tomb full of gold."

The sky above the Valley of the Kings turned from soft gray to pale blue. The sun had already risen above the eastern cliffs, but in the depths of the Valley, the shadows still clustered as Reis Gerigar and the crew of workers arrived. The day before, the men had removed the last of the ancient huts. Looking more like random heaps of rough stone, only an expert eye would have recognized them as the temporary living quarters of those who'd worked on the royal tombs. Today, with the huts gone, the workers planned on digging out the remaining three feet of rubble down to the bedrock.

Although Carter hadn't arrived yet, Reis Gerigar—one of the most respected and experienced foremen in Egypt—set the men to work. Picks and shovels scraped away.

An hour later, Carter arrived on donkey-back. He frowned. Why wasn't anyone working? Worry washed over him. There must have been an accident. Someone was hurt.

Reis Gerigar hurried forward, followed by a water boy. The boy had been playing, the foreman explained, "digging with sticks in the sand when suddenly he hit a hard surface." Digging harder, the boy had unearthed a stone step. The foreman swept his arm in the direction of the find.

Carter hurried to the spot where a ring of workmen had gathered. Yes, there it was, a creamy white stair. But did it lead to a royal tomb? Throwing off his jacket and grabbing up a pick, he began digging alongside the men.

As a second, then a third, then a fourth step appeared, it became clear to Carter that the style of the cutting was exactly that of a king's burial place. Royal tombs had steps cut down into the bedrock at the base of a cliff. When the desired depth was reached, a squared-off doorway gave entrance to the corridors and chambers of the tomb itself. But the door, Carter guessed, must still be well below-ground, since there was no sign of it yet.

"It is the tomb of the golden bird," one of the workmen declared. He, like some others, believed Carter's canary had indeed brought good luck.

As step after step emerged from the sand—eight, nine, ten—Carter felt both excitement and doubt. Did he dare hope? He and the men worked feverishly. All were eager to see what lay below. Still, the digging seemed to progress with agonizing slowness. As the day went on, a crowd grew around the excavation—tomb guards, guides, and curious tourists. Most didn't linger, for there was nothing much to see. But a few stayed to watch.

The sun was low in the west when the level of the twelfth step was reached. And there, before Carter, was the top of a doorway blocked with plastered stones. Obviously, some-one important was buried here. But who? He scanned the markings on the door, looking for a cartouche. This oval

The partially excavated door to the tomb. Difficult to see, but present, are ancient seal stamps made by the necropolis priests.

shape containing the hieroglyphic characters of a king's name would have told him whose tomb he'd found. But no cartouche was stamped into the upper part of the door. And Carter couldn't see the lower part because it was still hidden behind rubble.

"Anything, literally anything, might lie beyond that door," he later wrote, "and it took all my self control to keep from breaking down the doorway and investigating then and there."

But it was late in the day and the sun was setting. Besides, Carter was a professional. While treasure hunters like Theodore Davis might have broken down the door, Carter was a scientist. He would take a methodical approach. Photographs would have to be taken, and all the rubble sifted. After all, even the tiniest scraps of papyri could provide clues into the lives of ancient Egyptians. Carter had come this far. He would not cut corners.

But all of that would have to wait for Lord Carnarvon, who was still in England. In fairness, Carter could not take down the door or do any further excavation without his partner being present.

And so, summoning all his self-control, he had the men shovel the debris back into the stairwell. Only after the tomb was hidden once more, and he'd put guards on the site, did Carter finally ride home through the moonlight.

But first thing the next morning, he cabled Lord Carnarvon. "AT LAST HAVE MADE WONDERFUL DISCOVERY IN THE VALLEY. A MAGNIFICENT TOMB WITH SEALS INTACT . . . CONGRATULATIONS. CARTER."

And then?

He waited. In a state of excitement and suspense, he went about making preparations for the tomb's excavation. He ordered supplies and hired more workers. He sent a telegram to Arthur Callender, an engineer who lived in Egypt, asking if he would come to the Valley and help with the digging. And he wondered and worried. Had he found an intact tomb, or was it just another plundered burial site?

Three nerve-racking weeks later, on November 23, Lord Carnarvon and his lively twenty-year-old daughter, Evelyn, arrived at the excavation site. Already, the workmen had begun clearing the stairs once more. Carnarvon peered down into the ever-deepening pit. Was this it? Was this hole in the sand the culmination of his seven-year gamble in the Valley?

He would not find out that day. The sun was setting,

and despite everyone's eagerness to proceed, Carter sent the workers home for the night. They would begin digging again at first light.

The next morning, Lady Evelyn, Carnarvon, and Carter stood around the edge of the stairwell watching as step after step came into view. Despite the desert's early morning chill, Lord Carnarvon kept wiping his face on his sleeve, too overwrought to take out his silk handkerchief. Down below, the shape of a doorway lengthened. A steady stream of basket boys emerged, carrying out rubble. Tipping their loads far from the stairs, they went back for more.

The sun rose higher.

Carnarvon began pacing restlessly. Worried about his health, Evelyn tried to get her father to sit and drink some tea. Meanwhile, Carter, who'd remained aboveground with his patron, quivered like a hunting dog about to be released. Evelyn tried to get him to drink some tea, too.

Finally, just after lunchtime, Reis Gerigar called out. All sixteen stairs had been exposed and the doorway was clear.

Carter must have wanted to rush down the stairs. Instead, he offered his hand to Lady Evelyn, whose elegant but impractical black shoes had definitely *not* been made for tomb exploration. "Let's go down," he said calmly.

The view from the bottom of the staircase leading to the entrance passageway.

In an orderly fashion, the three descended into the hole.

Carter shone his flashlight across the door's plastered surface. Dozens of royal seals made by the necropolis priests had been stamped on the door. But the passage of time had made them hard to read. Who did this tomb belong to? Was there a king's name? If so, whose?

Carter knelt down with his flashlight to examine the lower portion of the door. Here there were a number of cartouches.

Posing on the tomb stairs are (from left to right) Lady Evelyn, Lord Carnarvon, Howard Carter, and Arthur Callender.

Tutankhamun's!

They'd found the tomb of the boy king! And they'd found it inside Carter's triangle just like he'd expected.

But their jubilation quickly turned to concern. The beams of Carter's flashlight revealed something else, too. He could tell by the ancient patches of plaster that a portion of the door had been opened and resealed, not once, but twice.

"Plunderers [have] entered it," said Carter. How much had been stolen? There was no way of knowing until they took down the door.

Carnarvon wanted to tear it down that instant. But Carter stopped him. The door had to be photographed first, and the seals and cartouches preserved if possible. It was proper archaeological procedure. They could not act hastily.

Not until the next day was the door carefully taken down. To the group's dismay, they found the passageway beyond completely filled with limestone chips. More dismaying was evidence that robbers had entered the tomb. Carter pointed it out: a tunnel obviously dug through the stone at the upper corner on the left side and then refilled. The archaeologist's concern turned to fear. Would they find the tomb ripped to shreds by ancient robbers? It seemed likely.

The workmen now began the tedious task of removing the stone chips. Every basketful had to be carefully examined. Whenever they found something—a strip of leather, a potsherd, a single faience bead—they had to stop digging so Carter could record the find. They discovered dozens of these sorts of artifacts. With the sun setting, there was still no end in sight. Another day came to a close without the excavators knowing exactly what they'd found.

Slowly, so, so slowly, the work continued the next morning.

The corridor lengthened.

Fifteen feet.

Twenty feet.

Twenty-five feet.

And then, around lunchtime, thirty feet into the corridor, workers came to a second doorway.

Carter's heart sank. This door also showed signs of having been broken through twice. He stood by nervously as the men took away the last of the debris blocking the second door. Then he shooed all the workers out. Just he and Carnarvon remained, along with Lady Evelyn and Arthur Callender. Carter and Carnarvon looked at each other. Neither could wait another moment. They had to know what lay on the other side. Hands trembling, Carter used an iron rod to make a tiny hole in the door's upper left-hand corner. "Darkness and black space as far as the testing iron could reach, showed that whatever lay beyond was empty and not filled like the passageway we had just cleared," Carter later wrote.

Widening the hole a little, he inserted a lit candle and looked in. At first, he could see nothing. A rush of hot air from the chamber beyond made the candle's flame flicker. But then his eyes adjusted and shapes began to emerge from the shadows. "Strange animals, statues and gold— everywhere the glint of gold."

Carter was speechless. He felt astonished, over-whelmed, delirious.

"Can you see anything?" Carnarvon asked anxiously.

Carter had trouble choking out his words. "Yes," he finally managed to say, "wonderful things."

It was said . . . the mummy's curse killed the golden bird.

As the excavators stood peering through the hole in the tomb's door, a messenger stumbled along the passageway. He brought news of a tragedy. A cobra had slipped into Carter's house, made its way into the drawing room, and coiled up the leg of the table where the birdcage sat. All that remained of the songbird, the messenger sadly reported, was a handful of golden feathers.

At that precise moment, a single ray of light from Carter's candle streaked through the door's hole and into the blackness beyond. It illuminated just one item—the head of a statue of the king. And wrapped around that head was the golden symbol of royalty and protection—the cobra!

The messenger gasped. It looked exactly like the serpent that had killed the bird. "An evil eye has been cast on the sweet bird . . . the bird that was [your] luck bringer," the man declared.

Carter replied that the lucky bird had *guided* them to this treasure. The cobras were just coincidental.

Was Carter right?

Or was the bird's death an evil omen?

Had Carter opened the tomb and unleashed the curse of Tutankhamun's mummy?

CHAPTER 6

Under Cover of Darkness
NIGHT OF NOVEMBER 26, 1922–
DECEMBER 1922

They came like those ancient robbers—Howard Carter, Lord Carnarvon, Lady Evelyn, and Arthur Callender—slipping in and out of the shadows along the Valley floor until they arrived at the tomb. The trusted workers guarding its entrance were surprised to see them. What were the excavators doing here in the middle of the night?

Just hours earlier they'd each taken a turn peeking through the hole Carter had made in the door. And each had seen wonders. Frustratingly, it had been too late in the day to explore further. And so, despite their excitement, the little group had closed the hole, locked the wooden grille that had been placed over the doorway, and ridden their donkeys to Carter's home in silence.

None of them could sleep. Long into the night, they talked about what they'd found. Did the sealed doorway lead directly to the sarcophagus and the pharaoh's mummy? Or was the doorway just the start of a long chain of rooms and galleries leading to the burial chamber? How much of the tomb had been plundered by ancient robbers? Had they gotten to the royal mummy? Anxiety and anticipation tightened around them.

It was probably Lady Evelyn's idea. Why not return to the tomb that very instant and take a look around? They *had* to know what they'd found. They just *had* to!

But sneaking back into the tomb was risky. The terms of their agreement with the Antiquities Service stated that a representative of the Service had to be present when an excavator entered a newly discovered tomb for the first time. To do otherwise violated the agreement. This meant the Antiquities Service could cancel their permission to dig in the Valley and take over excavation of the tomb. But that would only happen if the Antiquities Service found out they'd broken the rule. Did they want to chance it?

They did!

Silent as cats, they'd made their way back to the tomb. Carter unlocked the wooden grille. Then, in the wavering beam from his flashlight, he led the way down the stairs and along the passageway to the doorway. It took some time and effort, but eventually he made an opening big enough to wiggle through. Evelyn went first, followed by Carnarvon, then Callender, and, finally, Carter.

At first, they simply stood there in the dark chamber, breathing in the air of the pharaohs. Dust motes swam in the beam from their flashlights, and from time to time there came the smallest whisper of sound, as scraps of gold or a bit of cloth fell, disturbed by the entrance of air into the long-sealed chamber.

Did Carter feel as if he was trespassing? Although

A drawing of the moment Carter and the Carnarvons first explored the tomb, published in *Illustrated London News* in December 1923 and based on an interview Lord Carnarvon gave the artist.

almost three thousand years had passed since another human had stood in this spot, it must have seemed like only yesterday. A bouquet of flowers still lay on the threshold where a priest had put it, and a fingerprint could be seen on the inner painted surface of the door. The scent of oils and perfumes still lingered in the air.

Moving cautiously so as not to damage any artifacts,

The Antechamber of Tutankhamun's tomb looking toward the blocked, seal-stamped entrance to the burial chamber. Note the basket propped up against the wall, placed there by Carter to hide the entrance hole that he'd made during their secret midnight visit.

the four moved their flashlights from side to side. Looming out of the darkness were two ebony-black statues of a king with gold staffs, kilts, and sandals; gilded couches with the heads of strange beasts; exquisitely painted ornamental caskets; flowers; alabaster vases; strange black shrines adorned with a gilded monster snake; finely carved chairs; a golden throne; a heap of curious white egg-shaped boxes; stools of all shapes and designs; a scramble of overturned chariot parts glinting with gold; walking sticks. It was an incredible, mind-boggling, glorious mess, a confusion of priceless objects.

Uttering cries of delight and shaking their heads in wonder, Carnarvon and Lady Evelyn moved from statues to vases to shrines. They stood on tiptoe to see over the jumble and crouched to see under it. Suddenly, Lady Evelyn called out to the others. In the mess of objects she'd found a golden throne with figures of Tutankhamun and his queen, Ankhesenamun, depicted on the back. As the searchers stared at it, they felt deeply moved. The boy king was no longer myth; he was a living, breathing man with a wife who had surely mourned his death. "It is the most beautiful thing that has ever been found in Egypt," Carter declared.

While the others continued to lose themselves in the dazzling array of treasures, Carter systematically searched for traces of other doorways. He found one after lying on his stomach and shimmying under a couch that stood against the south wall. Peering through a hole obviously made by robbers, he saw into another chamber. Smaller than the one they were in, it was even more crammed with objects. Carter could tell that necropolis priests had not reordered the contents of this room. The "Annex," as Carter would come to call this space, was so jam-packed, he didn't attempt to go inside.

Instead he returned to the plastered and sealed doorway between the two ebony-black statues of a king. Examining it, he found a semicircle of discoloration, proof the robbers had breached this doorway, too, and that priests had repaired it. They hadn't done a good job. The hasty repairs were cracked and it didn't take long for Carter, with Callender's help, to remove enough of the door to slide feet-first into the chamber beyond.

Gold!

What looked like a solid wall of gold reached almost to the ceiling, and left only a narrow corridor alongside. Carter knew what it was—a funerary shrine. He was standing in the burial chamber—a sacred place.

He slipped around to the front of the shrine. He was met with the sight of two great gilded doors bolted

The cow-headed couch in the Antechamber under which Carter found this hole made by ancient robbers leading to the Annex.

shut and adorned with decorative hieroglyphs on a background of blue faience. As he examined the door, Carnarvon and Evelyn came up behind him. They'd left Callender in the first room, what would eventually be called the Antechamber. A stout man, he'd been unable to get through the hole.

Carnarvon urged Carter to open the doors.

Carter hesitated. This, he told the earl, was probably just the first of a number of golden shrines—one inside the other. Inside the shrines would be a sarcophagus. And inside the sarcophagus would be a coffin, or a number of coffins, inside which would rest the king's mummy. That is, he added, if robbers hadn't gotten to it first.

Carter placed his hand on the bolt. Should he?

Closing his fingers around it, he drew the bolt back. Then carefully . . . slowly . . . he opened the double doors. The ancient hinges creaked and Carter's light caught the curves of a delicate canopy sewn with golden rosettes—a funerary pall.

Beneath the pall was another set of double doors belonging to yet another shrine. These doors, too, were closed. Around their handles wound a cord upon which sat a dab of mud. This was the seal of the necropolis priests—a seal that was unbroken.

The linen pall with its golden rosettes would be one of the few artifacts that didn't survive the excavation. Workers accidentally left it outside the laboratory tomb during the off-season.

The seal was proof that robbers had not broken through the shrines. Did that mean the king was still there, undisturbed, as he had been for thousands of years? Carter desperately hoped so.

The burial chamber revealed one more surprise—a rectangular opening near the far corner leading to a fourth room filled, like the Antechamber and the Annex, with a fabulous jumble of artifacts. Eye and mind overwhelmed, Carter recalled only a few objects—a reclining statue of the jackal god Anubis, and behind it a golden chest with an

The mud seal (on the right of the handle) found intact on the cord of the third inner shrine.

exquisite statue of a goddess extending protective arms across it. Carter recognized this as the canopic chest containing the mummified remains of the king's stomach, intestines, lungs, and liver.

On the floor sat a life-sized golden head of the cow-headed goddess, Hathor. And there were more statues, more furniture, more boxes and chests of wood and ivory to be opened and examined. Carter would call this room the Treasury.

It was time to go. After wiggling out of the burial chamber, Carter, with Callender's help, replaced the blocks

Tutankhamun's royal viscera had multilayered protection. Inside this outer wooden shrine lay yet another gilded shrine, inside of which was a calcite chest. Nestled inside this chest were four canopic jars.

Three of Tutankhamun's four canopic jars, each fitted with a human head stopper and containing a tiny inlaid coffin. Inside each of these coffinettes lay a lovingly wrapped, carefully embalmed internal organ, either the boy king's liver, lungs, stomach, or intestines.

in the door and hid the hole they'd made with the lid of a big reed basket. Then they crossed the Antechamber and climbed through the opening in the inner doorway. Again, they disguised their break-in. In a state of disbelief, they made their way along the passageway and up the stairs. The cool air on their faces felt good after the dead and musty air in the tomb.

No one spoke as Carter relocked the wooden grille. The wonder of what they'd seen left them without words. They had done something no else had: found a royal tomb with most of its grave goods intact! Creeping back through the shadows, the four headed for home.

An Antiquities Service inspector was already waiting when the bleary-eyed group returned just hours later. Pretending they hadn't already been inside, they watched as workers pulled down the doorway leading into the Antechamber. It didn't take much acting skill to appear astonished. The sight of the artifacts still overwhelmed them. And the inspector, himself agog, didn't question their behavior. The group's nighttime adventure remained a secret.

But the tomb's discovery did not. Two days later, on November 29, the excavators held an official opening. They invited diplomats and commissioners, notables and officials both British and Egyptian. They also invited one member of the press, Arthur Merton, from the London *Times*. His exclusive report about the breathtaking find created an international sensation. Telegrams, letters, and messages from around the world rained down on the excavators. Meanwhile, an unruly throng of tourists began turning up at all hours. Many tried to sneak into the tomb. Others set up camp on the retaining wall workmen had built around the tomb's entrance. Gapers sat there all day, beneath the blazing sun, knitting, picnicking, and waiting for some dramatic event. But in those first few weeks, nothing much happened. So tourists took to huddling around the entrance. Staring down into the darkness, they listened for the muffled voices of the excavators. Any word thrilled them.

Carter found them as annoying as the swarms of flies in the Valley. He wished he could simply swat them away as he did the other pests. Instead, he resolved to ignore them. There were simply too many other things to think about.

Celebration gave way to serious discussion. One morning, as the men sat sipping coffee in the sunroom of Carter's house, the archaeologist gave his blunt appraisal of the work ahead: "This is going to take years."

After all, every single object had to be photographed and cataloged before being removed from the tomb. And many of the objects needed to be preserved first. Just the day before, an ancient necklace had crumbled at his touch, scattering hundreds of gold and faience beads across the rock-cut floor. Carter had spent hours on his hands and knees searching for and then picking up each tiny bead with a pair of tweezers. Afterward, he resolved that accidents like that would never happen again. Preservation would be his utmost priority.

Carnarvon was more concerned about cost. Clearing the tomb would be expensive. But it would be worth it. His agreement with the Antiquities Service stated that as

Tourists crowd around the entrance to the tomb, hoping for a glimpse of the treasures below.

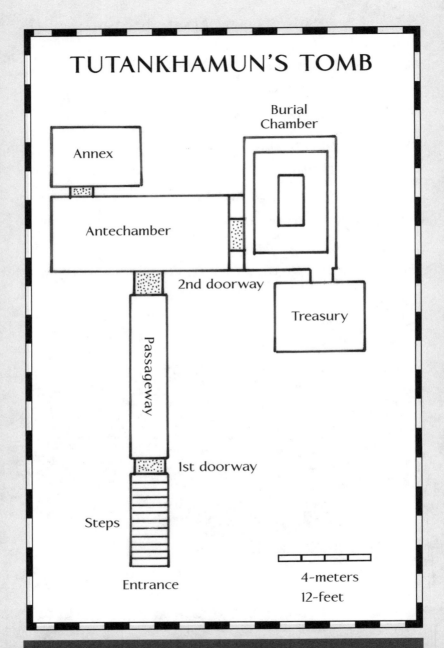

TUTANKHAMUN'S TOMB

Burial
Chamber

Annex

Antechamber

2nd doorway

Treasury

Passageway

1st doorway

Steps

Entrance

4-meters
12-feet

A diagram of Tutankhamun's tomb.

excavator he would get to keep half the tomb's contents. And half equaled a fortune.

Carter asked for extra staff, people who knew what they were doing. Just stabilizing the furniture would take weeks, as well as delicate hands. And then there were the clothes and the textiles and the jewelry.

Who did Carter have in mind?

He rattled off a list of names: Alfred Lucas, a chemist and expert on raw materials; Harry Burton, a photographer who worked for the Metropolitan Museum of Art; Arthur Mace, an archaeologist also from the Met; and Alan Gardiner, a linguist; as well as Egyptologists Percy Newberry and James Henry Breasted. All renowned experts, they were a superteam, perfect for this complicated job.

It would be weeks, however, before this team assembled and got to work.

In the meantime, Carter busied himself by having his men once again fill the tomb passageway with rock chips, and installing a thick door made of iron bars to fit the tomb's entrance. In two empty and little-visited tombs located close by, he set up a laboratory and a workroom. He ordered packing crates and wadding, rope and surgical bandages (to wrap around delicate objects), photographic materials and chemicals. He made endless to-do lists. He fretted and worried. He also bought another yellow canary.

Meanwhile, Carnarvon sailed home to England for the holiday season. Between parties and plum puddings, he visited Buckingham Palace, where he regaled King George V with tales of the discovery. And he spoke endlessly to reporters, who "pestered morning, noon and night" for details of the stunning discovery.

As Carter planned and Carnarvon celebrated, a political sandstorm was sweeping toward them. Since the end of World War I, the call "Egypt for Egyptians!" had grown louder and more insistent. By 1921, demonstrations in Cairo's streets had turned into strikes by transportation workers that turned into a national general strike, bringing Egypt to an economic standstill. Protest demonstrations spread across the country, sometimes erupting in violent riots. At first, the British had responded with their usual harshness—suppressing demonstrations and killing hundreds of protestors. Instead of folding, however, Egyptians defied the British and continued marching in the streets. Something had to be done to quiet the country. But what? For months, British politicians debated ways of placating the Egyptians while still keeping control of the country.

In February 1922, while Carter was still digging unsuc-
cessfully in the Valley of the Kings, the British declared
Egypt independent—that is, except in the matters of
defense and foreign affairs. Additionally, British forces
would remain on Egyptian soil. Many Egyptians called
out this independence as a sham. They rightly believed the
British would attempt to run the new government from
behind the scenes in ways that would remain in England's
best interest. Still, it *was* a step toward self-governance.
And so the two sides came together to begin drawing up a
constitution.

It was huge news—news that Carter and Carnarvon
for the most part ignored. What could independence
and an Egyptian constitution possibly have to do with
archaeology? Little did they know that these political
events—seemingly so far from the tomb—were about to
cause them big problems.

It was said . . . that the ghosts of ancient Egyptians tried to warn Lord Carnarvon.

A psychic named Cheiro told newspaper reporters all about it. It had happened, he claimed, on the very night the London *Times* reported the discovery of Tutankhamun's tomb. His story went like this:

He was sitting at the desk in his study when suddenly he shivered. Strange! Despite the blazing fire in the fireplace, the room had turned cold. And the electric lamp on his writing desk suddenly dimmed and glowed red. The psychic looked up from the letter he'd been writing.

No, it couldn't be!

But it was.

A shadowy form was taking shape. Slowly, it materialized into the ghost of a beautiful woman. Large, lustrous eyes shone from her noble face, while her hair was covered with a headdress of gold that reached to her shoulders. In the center of her forehead she wore a golden band shaped like a cobra, the symbol of Egyptian royalty.

An enormous scarab pinned a girdle of precious jewels around her slender waist.

Cheiro didn't doubt that the woman who stood before him was the spirit of an ancient Egyptian princess. But what did she want with him?

The spirit pointed to the psychic's writing pad.

Cheiro understood. He grabbed up his pencil. Over the next several minutes, he scribbled down the words that came into his mind. He felt as if he was taking dictation.

Eventually, his pencil slowed. The room warmed. Once again the lamp burned normally. The ghost vanished.

Cheiro read what he had written. It was a warning to Lord Carnarvon not to remove any relics from the cursed tomb. If he did, he would suffer from a swift and terrible sickness that would kill him.

"Rightly or wrongly, I sent this warning to Lord Carnarvon," Cheiro told reporters.

Was Cheiro telling the truth?

Did a curse hang over Lord Carnarvon's head?

CHAPTER 7

Early Days in the Tomb
JANUARY–MARCH 1923

On a chilly morning in late January 1923, Carter emerged from the tomb to see Lord Carnarvon and Lady Evelyn coming along the Valley floor. So they were back! Rolling down his shirtsleeves and pulling on his tweed jacket, Carter hurried to greet them.

Carnarvon looked around. So much had changed in the six weeks he'd been gone. Egyptian soldiers toting guns now guarded the site instead of workers shouldering pickaxes. Electric cables snaked across the ground and down into the tomb, powering the high-beam lamps that had been installed below. And three nearby tombs had been converted for various purposes. The tomb of Seti II was now a storeroom and laboratory. KV 55 had been transformed into a darkroom for developing

A group of Egyptian soldiers stand outside the tomb, 1923.

photographs. And the tomb of Ramesses XI was being used as the "luncheon room."

Carter showed the earl and his daughter around. As he did, Carnarvon peppered him with questions. How was Carter keeping track of each object?

Systematically, of course. The archaeologist explained his exacting method. His system required numbering *everything*—every bead, every scrap, every object. Once numbered, the item was sketched *and* photographed. Each object was then plotted on a map of the tomb, recording exactly where it had been found. Additionally, Carter wrote a detailed description of each object on a numbered record card. He added these cards to his official index.

Carter's scientific team (left to right): Arthur Callender, Arthur Mace, Harry Burton, Howard Carter, Alan Gardiner, and Alfred Lucas.

And how were the objects being removed from the tomb?

Again, systematically. Starting in the Antechamber, objects were removed one by one, and from north to south. There were difficulties. The huge, animal-shaped funerary couches would have to be broken apart because they were too big to fit in the passageway. And the bits of gold decorating the jumble of chariots were just barely clinging to the ancient wood. It would take weeks of conservation work before any of these items could be moved. Meanwhile, chemist Alfred Lucas had begun unpacking

Some of the Egyptian men who worked at the tomb. While the British photographer who took this picture in early 1923 did not bother to record their names, he did identify the three in back as "head men."

the dozens of storage chests. Each was chock-full of every-thing from jewelry to clothing—sandals, beaded robes, loincloths. Even the king's sidelock had been found in one of the chests. The discovery of this long braid of hair worn by him as a child especially thrilled Carter. Had it been included in his tomb goods for sentimental rea-sons? he wondered. Or was it simply that all items used by a king—even his hair—were routinely saved for inclusion in his burial? Like the chariots and the clothing, it would require a delicate touch and careful conservation.

Would Carnarvon and his daughter like to see some of these conservation efforts?

Carter led them to the tomb laboratory. The three could smell the chemicals—acetone, paraffin, celluloid solution, and beeswax—while they were still walking up the path. Inside, shelves and wooden tables had been set up. A small bronze statue, recently conserved and cleaned, sat on one of these tables. Carnarvon thought it looked more beautiful than when he first had laid eyes on it. He clapped Carter on the back. Well done!

Lady Evelyn suggested a toast to celebrate it all.

But Carter declined. He had so much to do. Excusing himself, he hurried back to the tomb.

In the laboratory tomb, Arthur Mace (standing) and Alfred Lucas conserve one of the black-and-gold statues from the tomb's Antechamber, 1923.

Howard Carter escorts a gilt-and-inlaid box to the laboratory tomb. Inside he would find two adzes, a glove, a faience collar, and a leopard-skin robe.

And so, in the shade of the luncheon tomb, Evelyn and her father toasted by themselves.

The painted wooden box with scenes of the boy king in his chariot emerged from the darkness of the tomb, carried by workers on a padded stretcher. As the morning sunlight touched it for the first time in three thousand years, shouts of delight rose from the crowd gathered at the entrance. The clicking of cameras rattled like hail. Reporters hurled questions at Carter as he hurried alongside it.

He didn't answer them. Instead, he shouted for everyone to stand back.

The bearers headed along the path toward the tomb laboratory.

Spectators followed after them, staring and stumbling and trying to get a better look at the lovely object. Nothing like that chest had ever been seen before. And it was just one of thousands of glorious artifacts that would eventually emerge from belowground.

No wonder the world was fascinated by the discovery. Every facet of the story—the history, the hidden treasure, the ancient spells and magic—excited the public. They clamored for details. In response, newspapers from all over the world sent reporters and photographers to the Valley. But members of the press soon discovered they'd been excluded from reporting firsthand on the tomb. While in London, Lord Carnarvon, eager to recoup some of the fortune he was spending on the excavation, had signed a contract giving the London *Times* the exclusive right to publish all official stories about the discovery. This meant that Carnarvon only gave interviews and photographs to the *Times*. Reporters working for any other newspapers had to pay the *Times* for use of this exclusive material, and they had to publish it a day late.

Arthur Callender (left) and Howard Carter carefully carry pieces of a chair from the tomb. Using a stretcher to transport artifacts minimized touching by human hands and thus possible damage.

This arrangement infuriated reporters, especially Egyptian ones. "It is an unheard of thing that the Egyptian papers should have to take all the news of an archaeological discovery in Egypt from London newspapers," they complained. They, like other reporters, had to content themselves with secondhand stories, or gossip overheard in the dining room of the Winter Palace Hotel. None of this gave them enough material to satisfy their readers' growing fascination with all things Tutankhamun. And so they began spinning tales about ancient Egypt, its magical spells, incantations, and prayers. Some even retold the stories about the cursed coffin lid of the priestess of Amen-Ra. Readers ate it up.

Within weeks of Carnarvon's return, all the artifacts had been cleared from the Antechamber except for the two tall statues standing guard at the entrance to the burial chamber. Carter had left them on purpose, knowing they would create a dramatic setting for the special event he and Carnarvon were planning: the official opening of the burial chamber. Invitations had already been sent to forty privileged guests, including the tough new director of the Antiquities Service, Pierre Lacau. A distinguished-looking man with white hair and beard, he was so precise in his habits that people said he made lists of lists. And he was about to play an important part in the tomb's story.

On the afternoon of February 17, 1923, aristocrats, politicians, and other officials, including Lacau, arrived in the Valley. After dining in the luncheon tomb, they headed to Tutankhamun's tomb. As they neared the entrance, they had to pick their way through a forest of camera tripods set up by the many reporters.

The reporters shouted questions. What was happening? Surely the presence of all these VIPs meant something extraordinary was about to take place.

"We are going to have a concert, Carter is going to sing a song," replied Carnarvon impishly. He refused to answer any questions. As per his agreement, only Arthur Merton of the London *Times* would be allowed the scoop.

One by one, the guests removed their coats and descended into the gloom.

Filing along the passageway, they came to the Antechamber. Rows of chairs had been set up for them, and a raised platform had been built between the two statues standing guard at the entrance to the burial chamber. It looked like a stage. In fact, it had been built to hide the place where Carter and the others had entered months earlier. Still, both men were a bit nervous that someone would find out they'd already been inside the chamber. It was best to start knocking down the wall soon. Under the glare of two electric lights, and with a trembling hand, Carter began chiseling away at the top of the door.

The guests fell silent, transfixed.

Within a few minutes, he'd made a hole big enough to shine a flashlight through. He directed its beam into the darkness beyond.

Behind him, the guests shifted eagerly in their seats.

"I see a wall of gold-and-blue faience!" Carter finally said. It was, of course, the side of the outer shrine that he'd seen months earlier.

Lady Evelyn gave an excited cry.

After that, the going got harder. With the help of several workers, Carter removed the giant blocks of stone that made up the door. An hour passed. Then another. The tomb grew hot and close. Its air felt heavy with suspense. At last, everyone could see what had been hidden behind the door—a huge gilt shrine meant to protect the mummy in its sarcophagus.

When the hole was big enough, Carter dropped down into the burial chamber. Lord Carnarvon quickly followed, as did Pierre Lacau, who refused to let them go without him. The men carefully edged their way along the

Howard Carter (left) stands just inside the mostly removed doorway between the Antechamber and the burial chamber in this photograph taken at the official opening in February 1923. Arthur Callender stands beside him on the wooden platform built for the occasion. The side of the outer shrine is barely visible through the doorway.

narrow space between the shrine and the rock-cut wall. At the corner of the shrine, Carter found an exquisite alabaster vase. He did not remember it from his earlier visit. He didn't remember seeing the wick lamp with the small mud base, either. He picked it up to examine it closer. Its hieroglyphic text read: "It is I who hinder the sand from choking the secret chamber. I am for the protection of the deceased."

The first outermost shrine was so big it filled almost the entire burial chamber, as this photograph shows.

A curse?

No, it was a common protection spell. Its purpose truly was to guard against encroaching sand.

For half an hour Carter, Carnarvon, and Lacau left the other guests sitting in a stew of anxiety as they revisited the chamber. The electric lights from the Antechamber made it easier to see than last time. On the floor on the far side of the shrine, eleven oars were carefully laid out—the magic oars the king would need to ferry himself across the waters of the underworld. And in one corner, wrapped in reeds, they found a silver trumpet. Carter believed it had been used to summon the pharaoh's troops. Despite its tarnish, he felt sure that if blown, the instrument would "fill the Valley with a resounding blast."

Finally, Carnarvon and Lacau emerged from the burial chamber. They said not a word to the guests, just raised their hands in amazement at what they'd seen. Then they invited the others to go in, two at a time. Carter, who'd remained in the burial chamber to guide them, enjoyed the line of dazed, delighted expressions.

Meanwhile, the left-out reporters huddled around the tomb entrance and speculated about what was happening below. One of them cornered a workman. He told the reporter that three mummies had been found. This was

The narrow gap between the north wall of the burial chamber and the outermost shrine with wooden paddles and other ritual objects in position. The numbers beside the artifacts were placed there by Carter as part of his method of keeping track of discoveries.

contradicted minutes later by another worker who said that eight mummies had been found. By midafternoon, word leaked out that a giant cat statue had been discovered. Reporters rushed to telegraph these details back to their newspapers. Too late, they discovered that none of it was true. Their grumbling against Carnarvon and his deal with the London *Times* grew even louder.

Three hours after they'd descended into the tomb, the VIPs filed out of the tomb, hot, dusty, and awed. "For the first time in all my experience," said one, "I felt the presence of the dead."

The days grew hotter. In the tomb the temperature soared to 104 degrees some afternoons. Dust storms became a daily occurrence. Carter knew the Egyptian summer would soon force him to close down the site for the season. Frantic, his nerves frayed, he pressed on day and night. Recording. Conserving. Packing. There was just so much to do!

The constant parade of visitors didn't help. Since the opening of the burial chamber, royalty, famous Egyptians, visiting dignitaries, and friends of Carnarvon arrived at the tomb expecting a private tour. How could Carter say no to the queen of Belgium or a British viscount or a member of the Egyptian royal family? Grudgingly, because each arrival interrupted their work, one of the team members took the visitor around. "This afternoon I had standing around me . . . an earl, a lady, a sire and two honorables. A beastly nuisance they are too, and I wish they'd keep away," complained Arthur Mace.

Sometimes the nuisances turned ridiculous, such as the visit from a portly British general. While squeezing through the entrance to the burial chamber, he got stuck. It took four men, pushing and pulling, to free him. He came loose, remarked one of the rescuers, "with a noise like a champagne cork."

Much to Carter's dismay, worldwide interest in the discovery grew with each object that moved along the path to the laboratory tomb. Each day brought greater crowds to the tomb. Movie cameras whirred. Newspaper cameras clicked. Carter felt ready to jump out of his skin. "No power on earth could shelter us from the light of publicity," he grumbled.

Then there was the question of ownership of the treasures. Should they be shared between Carnarvon and the Egyptian government, as stated in the concession, or should all the objects go to the museum in Cairo? This question had suddenly become entangled with Egypt's struggles to gain its independence from Great Britain. Daily there were anti-British strikes and protests in Cairo and Luxor. Egyptians claimed the tomb's treasures as their own, and demanded they stay in Egypt. They saw the treasures as a central symbol of their national identity. The days when a European queen could deck herself out in the jewels of an ancient Egyptian queen, or a millionaire American could use the skull of an ancient prince as a paperweight, were over, they declared. The tomb and everything in it belonged to the Egyptians, and to the Egyptians alone. Foreigners no longer had any right to it.

Pierre Lacau had been thinking along these same lines. He'd long resented the wealthy foreigners who—for a price—dug where and when they wanted, and took whatever they wanted. He'd taken over the Antiquities Service with the firm intention of keeping everything discovered for Egypt. No longer would diggers get half of everything they found. No longer would national treasures leave the country. All of Tutankhamun's treasures must stay put.

And so, just days after the public opening of the burial chamber, Lacau summoned Carnarvon to his office in the Cairo museum.

The director got to the point. He reminded Carnarvon of a clause in their agreement: The contents of an intact tomb belonged entirely to the Egyptian government.

Carnarvon countered by reminding Lacau that Tutankhamun's tomb had not been found intact. Ancient robbers had "ransacked" it twice.

"Rifled," corrected Lacau. Certainly, some oils and a few pieces of jewelry had been taken. But the king's body had not been touched, as the unbroken seal on the bolt of the second shrine seemed to prove. So technically, the director concluded, the tomb was intact.

An incensed Carnarvon rose from his chair. He'd spent vast amounts of money in his sixteen years of excavating with Carter. He'd financed these digs with the understanding that he would keep half of whatever was found. How dare Lacau change the rules now! He vowed to take the Antiquities Service to court if necessary.

His fury stayed with him all the way back to the excavation site. There he stomped and complained and wrote letter after angry letter to government officials.

All these pressures—the overwhelming amount of work, the constant interruptions by visitors, the political rumbling of Egyptian nationalists, and Lacau's decision—took their toll. Carnarvon grew irritable. Carter grew more short-tempered than usual. Everyone working at the site felt overheated and pressured.

On a sweltering afternoon toward the end of February, Carter returned to his house to find Carnarvon pacing in the sitting room. Within moments a shouting match erupted. What did the two men argue about? No one knows. But it ended with bitter words on both sides. Carter, in a rage, ordered his partner to leave . . . and never come back! It was obvious the men needed a break from the tomb, the press, the public, *and* each other.

Five days later, Carter closed up the tomb for the season. Although he still had work to do in the laboratory, he holed up in his house for a few days. He saw no one and went nowhere. He reveled in being alone.

This photo of Lord Carnarvon standing in a doorway was taken just weeks before he fell ill.

Carnarvon, too, escaped. Along with Evelyn, he cruised up the Nile, visiting temples around Aswan and letting the river breezes restore him. His mind, however, kept returning to his argument with Carter. He deeply regretted it. Over the years, the men had grown close, and he'd come to think of Carter as his dearest friend. And so he wrote him a heartfelt letter:

> *I have been feeling very unhappy today, and I do not know what to think, or do . . . I have no doubt that I have done many foolish things and I am very sorry . . . There is only one thing I have to say to you that I hope you will always remember—whatever your feelings are or will be for me in the future, my affection for you will never change.*

If Carter wrote back, there is no record of it.

Break over, Carter and his team resumed work in the laboratory tomb. Dozens of objects still remained on the tables, waiting to be stabilized, wrapped, and crated up for the boat ride to Cairo.

Carnarvon returned, too. But the work was too meticulous and scientific for him to help. Instead, he pottered around the lab, pestering the team with questions and getting in their way. Grumbled Arthur Mace, "It takes us all we know to restrain Carnarvon from plunging into things he shouldn't." The team even took to finding him little jobs to keep him from "mooning around," like "arranging the pendants of a collar, which [kept] him out of mischief for a long time."

Carter wished Carnarvon would just go back to the Winter Palace, and stay there. The earl certainly looked as if he could use the rest. While in Aswan, he had been bitten on the cheek by a mosquito. By the time he arrived back in the Valley, he had nicked the bite while shaving. But it wasn't the wound that concerned Carter. It appeared to be healing nicely. No, it was Carnarvon's fatigue, his ghostlike pallor, and—most worrisome—his teeth. Every few days one of them chipped, or fell out of his mouth. Carnarvon blamed these symptoms on heat and stress. He didn't connect them to the wound on his cheek. But they *were* related, dangerously so. Unknown to the earl, a terrible infection was creeping through his bloodstream.

With nothing to do at the work site, Carnarvon decided to return to Cairo. He planned on pressing Lacau harder about dividing the tomb objects. But he and Evelyn had just checked into their rooms at the Continental-Savoy Hotel when he complained of feeling "rather poorly." A doctor was immediately called. He advised bed rest.

Evelyn did not leave her father's side. Hour after hour,

she soothed his fevered brow with a damp cloth, spooned broth between his parched lips, and read aloud his favorite poems. She tried not to show her fear. But in truth, she was deeply worried. While her father's health had never been good since his car accident, Egypt's climate had always made him feel better. Why not this time? She admitted her fears to Carter in a March 17 letter. "The old man is very seedy," she wrote. "All the glands in his neck are swelling . . . and he has a high temperature." Scared and alone, she ended her letter, "I wish . . . you were here."

Making this situation worse was the overzealous press. Carnarvon was big news, and the moment reporters learned he was in Cairo, they'd congregated outside his hotel. They hoped he'd come out and say something, *anything*, about the tomb. But as days passed without Carnarvon stepping foot outside, newspapermen grew suspicious. They pelted other hotel guests with questions. Had they seen Lord Carnarvon? Was someone at the hotel ill? Who had the doctor visited that morning?

It didn't take long for the details of Carnarvon's illness to leak out. And it gave the excavation story a new angle. His illness, coming at the very moment of his triumph, riveted readers around the world.

What would happen next?

It was said . . . that the mummy's curse was causing Carnarvon's illness.

The bestselling author of occult novels Marie Corelli had made this discovery. And she wrote a letter to the *New York World* telling readers all about it. The letter, published on the front page of the newspaper on March 24, 1923, began: "I see the hand of the pharaoh rather than a bite of a mosquito in his illness." Why did she believe this? Because, she explained, on her shelves sat a rare and ancient book titled *The Egyptian History of the Pyramids*. And within its dusty pages she'd come across a long-forgotten passage containing a warning. Anyone entering a sealed tomb, it said, would suffer "the most dire punishment." Had not Carnarvon invaded the sacred space of a pharaoh? Had he not removed that pharaoh's treasures, the very items needed to journey to the afterlife?

"That is why I ask," concluded Corelli. "Was it a mosquito bite that has so seriously infected Lord Carnarvon?"

Or was it something more sinister?

Was it a curse?

CHAPTER 8

And at the Continental-Savoy Hotel . . .

MARCH–APRIL 1923

Lord Carnarvon's loved ones rushed to his bedside. His son, Lord Porchester, set sail from India. His wife, Lady Almina, took off from London. And Carter hurried from the Valley of the Kings. Within days, they were all gathered around him. In their presence, Carnarvon rallied. He ate a bit and sat up in bed. His doctors, however, did not expect him to recover. Five years before the discovery of antibiotics, there was little they could do except wait and see as the infection continued to spread. Carnarvon accepted his fate. "I have heard the call," he told his family. "I am preparing."

On April 4, Lord Carnarvon's health took a turn for the worse. His fever raged, and his breathing became ragged.

The Continental-Savoy Hotel in Cairo where Lord Carnarvon died.

Delirious, he muttered over and over, "A bird is scratching at my face. A bird is scratching at my face."

Was the dying earl talking about the ancient Egyptian belief that Nekhbet, the vulture goddess, would scratch the face of anybody who dared disturb the peace of a pharaoh's tomb? Or were his words simply due to the imaginings of his fevered mind? Like his father, Lord Porchester believed in the occult. His father's muttering must have caused him to shudder with fear.

Hours passed. Then just after midnight on April 5, 1923, Carnarvon opened his eyes and reportedly said, "Pharaoh, I am returning to you." Then he lapsed into unconsciousness.

Lady Almina held her husband's hands. At 1:45 a.m.—just four months after discovering Tutankhamun's tomb—Lord Carnarvon breathed his last.

It was said . . . that at that exact moment, all the lights in Cairo flickered.

Then . . . SNAP!

The whole city plunged into tomb-like darkness.

At that moment, at Highclere Castle, Lord Carnarvon's favorite fox terrier, Susie, howled inconsolably and dropped over dead.

And at that moment, in the Valley of the Kings, a guard at the excavation site jerked to attention. He saw a scattering of dust. He heard a skittering of pebbles. Someone was walking around the tomb! Shouldering his rifle, he rushed to investigate.

He found nothing.

All he heard was the gusting of the wind.

CHAPTER 9

Curses!

APRIL–JUNE 1923

Lord Carnarvon's death caused newspapers both in Egypt and abroad to go "curse crazy." Had some dark and ancient power caused his death? Readers around the world were now as transfixed by these stories as they were by the tomb's excavation. The psychic Cheiro made headlines when he told the press about the warnings he'd received from the spirit world. So did Carnarvon's dying words—"A bird is scratching at my face"—when newspapers reported them. "The Earl could have been referring only to that protectoress of death, Nekhbet, the vulture goddess," declared London's *Daily Mail*.

Curse stories abounded. In one account, Carter reportedly found a clay tablet above the tomb's entrance that read: "Death will slay with its wings whoever disturbs the peace of the pharaoh." Fearing the written warning would scare away any superstitious workers, Carter decided to destroy all traces of it. And so he rode out into the desert and, under the light of a midnight moon, buried it deep within the Sahara sand. There was, of course, no record of this tablet in the excavation's index—no photographs and no notes. In truth, the tablet never existed.

But that didn't stop the press. Another story reported on the wick lamp Carter had found in the burial chamber. This account correctly quoted the inscription on its base: "It is I who hinder the sand from choking the secret chamber. I am for the protection of the deceased." But the reporter then added his own fictional line: "And I will kill all those who cross into the sacred precincts of the royal king who lives for ever." He obviously thought it made a better story.

A further inscription was reportedly found on the back of a statue near the burial chamber. "It is I who drive back robbers of the tomb with flames of the desert. I am the protector of Tutankhamun's grave." This, too, was made up. No such inscription existed.

Still, the stories spread.

When a tourist who'd visited the tomb weeks earlier was struck and killed by a taxi in Cairo, newspapermen blamed it on the curse.

When an overweight associate curator of Egyptology at the British Museum dropped dead from a heart attack, newspapermen blamed it on the curse.

When an elderly Egyptologist at Paris's Louvre Museum died in his sleep, newspapermen blamed it on the curse.

Was it so hard to believe a curse was at work? Lots of people had read about the coffin lid of the priestess of Amen-Ra. And many had been convinced by these stories. Additionally, the idea that the ancient Egyptians with their magical spells and mystical burial rituals had possessed some secret and powerful source of long-forgotten knowledge was a popular one. This didn't seem such an impossible idea when so many other seemingly magical things were happening in the world. Newfangled inventions like telephones, phonographs, radios, and movie cameras allowed voices and images to move through wires and tubes. Airplanes allowed people to fly. The world was becoming a more scientific place. So it stood to reason that modern, scientific Egyptologists might soon unlock those age-old secrets. They might possibly solve the mysteries of life, death, and immortality, too. Perhaps the veil between the living and the dead would finally be lifted.

Talking with the dead was another popular idea at the

time of the tomb's discovery. Up to sixteen million people had died in World War I (1914–1918) and another fifty to one hundred million worldwide had died in the flu pandemic that followed (1918–1920). Almost everyone had a loved one who'd recently died. And these losses led to an increased fascination with the occult. People desperately wanted to communicate with the departed. Séances, palm readers, and psychics grew in popularity. And so did interest in ancient Egyptian religion. All those spells and rituals must surely be a way to connect with the dead. Scientists just hadn't figured out how they worked yet.

And *that's* what made the opening of Tutankhamun's tomb so dangerous, many believed. Because Carter didn't understand the chamber's true powers, he'd accidentally unleashed a vengeful spirit into the world. His *not* knowing had reawakened the pharaoh's mummy. And now innocent victims would pay the price.

Readers panicked. In England, people packed up every scrap of Egyptian antiquity they owned—potsherds, scarabs, statuettes, anything—and shipped them to the British Museum. Most of these items had little value and would have been returned by museum workers if the parcels had included return addresses. Most did not. After all, senders were hoping to shift any curses from themselves to the museum. The last thing they wanted back was that mummified hand . . . or canopic jar . . . or string of faience beads.

Meanwhile, in the United States, several politicians called for a congressional investigation into the mummies on display in American museums. Were they as dangerous as the objects from Tutankhamun's tomb? Not surprisingly, Congress chose not to act.

As for Howard Carter, one afternoon, a group of reporters surrounded him. Did Carter believe in the curse? Did he fear for his own life?

Still mourning the loss of his friend, Carter snapped, "It is too much to believe that some [ghost] is keeping watch . . . over the dead pharaoh, ready to wreak vengeance on anyone who goes too near. All sane people should dismiss such ridiculous inventions."

Other Egyptologists agreed. Responding to all the sensational—and fake—news stories, Wallis Budge, keeper of the Egyptian antiquities at the British Museum, simply exclaimed, "Bunkum!"

If there really were curses on ancient tombs, added his assistant H. R. Hall, "there would not be any archaeologists [alive] today."

These logical arguments made no difference. Finally the world's press had a story they didn't have to go to the

London *Times* for. And it was far more exciting than the slow-moving events at the tomb. Yes, indeed, the curse sold newspapers.

Eleven days after Carnarvon's death, Carter returned to the Valley. He looked, said Arthur Mace, "rather tired and washed out. He must have had an awful time."

Carter kept his grief to himself. The loss of his friend was beyond measure. They should have been planning the opening of the sarcophagus together. They should have been shoulder to shoulder when the face of the king was finally revealed. But now Carter was alone. He dulled his sadness by throwing himself into work.

Hundreds of last-minute details required his attention before closing the tomb for the season. Already the excavation team had photographed, recorded, and preserved the last of the artifacts in the laboratory tomb. Now Carter rolled up his white-sleeved shirt. With temperatures inside the makeshift lab soaring to 120 degrees most days, he carefully packed all the artifacts that had been removed just from the Antechamber—more than five hundred of them—into crates for the barge ride to the Cairo museum. Once there, he uncrated each object and placed them in cases for display.

Egyptian porters use the hand-propelled railway to take the wooden-crated tomb objects to the Nile at the end of the first season.

Did Carter notice the excitement in the streets? Egyptian men packed Cairo's coffeehouses and buzzed about the news: A constitution had been announced and it provided for elections! Soon men (the right was not extended to women) would get to vote for representatives to the very first Egyptian parliament. The men debated candidates. Would they vote for high-ranking Egyptians backed by the British? Or would they vote for Nationalists, men who championed Egypt's complete political independence? Only time and ballots would tell.

Meanwhile, his job at the museum complete, Carter boarded a ship bound for England. But he would be back in October. After all, only about a fourth of the excavation was finished. The shrines still had to be dismantled and the sarcophagus opened. Was the mummy intact?

Egyptian porters load crates of tomb treasures onto a government barge that will take them to the museum in Cairo.

That, too, remained to be discovered. Then there was the Annex—the little room off the Antechamber—with its jumble of artifacts. And the Treasury, located off the burial chamber. It so glittered with gold that Carter had been forced to put a sheet of plywood over the entrance so he wouldn't be tempted to excavate that room first. That would *not* have been systematic and methodical. But why think about all this now? Carter looked forward to a few months of rest.

Tutankhamun's mummy lay undisturbed for one more summer.

It was said . . . the mummy's curse took its revenge on more victims.

George Jay Gould, a wealthy American financier, toured the tomb in 1923. Almost immediately afterward, he fell sick with a fever and persistent cough. Wanting to be treated by a lung specialist, he'd traveled to the French Riviera. But his health did not improve. Instead, with each passing day he grew weaker.

Reporters buzzed around the villa where Gould was staying. What was the American's diagnosis? No one would say. "Considerable mystery surrounds the nature of his complaint," reported the *New York Times*. Was the American another victim of the mummy's curse?

Inside the villa, Gould's loved ones gathered around his sickbed. As the dying man struggled for breath, he claimed to be surrounded by the "spirits of the pharaohs," and that Anubis, the Egyptian god of mummification and the afterlife, "drew the last breath out of him."

Gould died on May 16, 1923. Was he a victim of the curse?

Hugh Gerard Evelyn-White was an eminent archaeologist who visited the tomb right after it was discovered in 1922. Some people speculated he might even have briefly helped with the excavation. Its discovery certainly thrilled him, at least until he began to hear workers muttering about the curse. A few even claimed they'd seen the spirit of the jackal-headed god, Anubis, in the tomb's passageway. Their whisperings shook Evelyn-White to the core.

Not long afterward, he went home to London.

Not long after that, he hanged himself.

His death on September 9, 1924—almost a year and a half after Carnarvon died—was considered mysterious by the press. According to the London *Times*, Evelyn-White's suicide note read, "I knew there was a curse on me." But other versions differed. According to one report, he left this chilling message written in his own blood: "I have succumbed to a curse which forces me to disappear."

In the spring of 1923, handsome, wealthy Ali Kamel Fahmy Bey visited the tomb. While touring the burial chamber, he joked about the curse. He even wondered aloud if his presence in the tomb would make him one of its victims.

Reporters claimed it did. Just months after his visit, on July 11, 1923, his wife of six months shot him in their London hotel room. Wounded, he was taken to the hospital. Hours later, he died.

The curse, declared newspapers, had struck again.

Who would be next?

CHAPTER 10

Shrines, Sarcophagus, and Coffins
NOVEMBER 1923–JUNE 1924

The clanking of picks and shovels broke the Valley of the Kings's silence. Carter watched as the workmen again removed the seventeen hundred tons of fill that had covered the tomb's stairway during the off-season. Although it was November, the cliffs surrounding the Valley were partly obscured by haze and quivering heat waves as the temperature soared to 100 degrees.

Spirits soared, too. Basket boys scampered eagerly up and down the stairs, carrying off sand and small stones. Workers chatted and laughed. Some even burst into song. Carter must have wished he felt as glad-hearted. But since his arrival in Egypt, things had been difficult.

First there was the matter of the concession. Although the Antiquities Service had allowed Lord Carnarvon's widow, Almina, to take over, the issue of who owned the

The team returned to the excavation site, too, and even though Carnarvon was gone, his taste for the finer things remained, as this photo taken in the dining tomb proves. Every day, lunch was brought from the Winter Palace and served on china, crystal, and white tablecloths by Egyptian waiters. The diners are (left to right): James H. Breasted (archaeologist), Harry Burton (photographer), Alfred Lucas (chemist), Arthur Callender (engineer), Arthur Mace (archaeologist), Howard Carter, and Alan Gardiner (linguist).

treasure remained. Would Lord Carnarvon's estate receive any portion of it? Would Lacau insist on keeping every object for Egypt? Carter felt sure those questions would only be answered after a lengthy court battle.

Then there was the constant stream of tourists, reporters,

government officials, dignitaries, VIPs, *everyone* around the tomb. Carter had demanded that the Antiquities Service (who handled all requests for visits to the tomb) limit the number of visitors. So far, he'd heard nothing back from Director Lacau. This both annoyed and worried Carter. His scientific work would be slowed—maybe even stopped—if parades of people were allowed to tromp all around.

And finally, there was Lacau's recent and upsetting attitude toward the excavation. This season he had imposed a new rule: An inspector from the Service must always be present to oversee work at the site. He had also demanded a list of all members of the excavation team for the Antiquities Service approval.

Offended, Carter had tried to argue. How dare the Service meddle in *his* excavation? But Lacau had snapped back, "The government no longer discusses but informs you of its decisions."

Carter was taken aback . . . and infuriated. Without Lord Carnarvon's clout and diplomatic skills to help smooth things over, his relations with the government were unraveling.

It was a less than promising start to the season.

*   *   *

Working in cramped space, Howard Carter (center), Arthur Callender (far right), and two workmen remove the roof section of the outer shrine, December 1923.

The hammering and pounding of workmen soon disturbed the peace of the tomb. Under Carter's supervision, they tore down the wall separating the Antechamber from the burial chamber. Then they built wooden scaffolding and an elaborate series of chain hoists for lifting heavy loads. Under the glaring electric lights, Carter and his team members began dismantling the outer shrine. In such a confined space, they constantly bumped their heads and pinched their fingers as they eased apart the three-thousand-year-old pieces of wood. "We had to squeeze

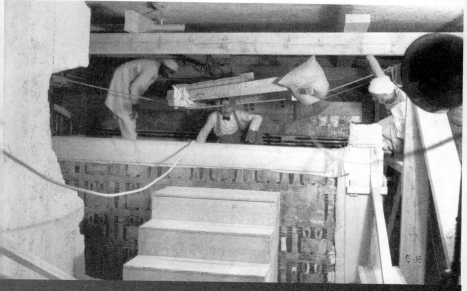

Howard Carter (center) and two workmen rig scaffolding above the outermost shrine. Along with lifts and hoists, their contraption included padding and even a pillow to keep people from smashing their heads on the rock ceiling of the burial chamber.

Wedged between ceiling and outermost shrine, Howard Carter (center) along with Arthur Callender and an unnamed worker roll away the funeral pall.

in and out like weasels," recalled Carter, "and work in all kinds of embarrassing positions."

It took weeks, but at last the outer shrine had been removed. The excavation team crowded into the burial chamber to watch as Carter carefully rolled back the fragile rosette-strewn funerary pall that covered the second shrine. Then he slipped back the bolts at the top and bottom of the second shrine, cut the sealed cord, and swung back the doors on their ancient hinges.

The men peered inside.

The doors of a third shrine winked back at them in golden splendor.

Carter could see that they, too, were bolted and sealed.

He paused. The excavation should proceed scientifically. That is, the team should remove the second shrine before peering into the third. But Carter could not contain his excitement. He had to see what lay within that third shrine.

With surprising ease, he opened its doors.

There glimmered a fourth shrine covered with hieroglyphs. Percy Newberry, the Egyptology expert, leaned in for a closer look. He ran his finger along a line of script. Then he whispered its meaning: "I have seen yesterday; I know tomorrow."

All fell silent for a moment.

Howard Carter crouches before the open shrine doors as an awestruck Arthur Callender and an unnamed worker peer over his shoulder.

The first glimpse of the sarcophagus filling the entire space of the fourth (innermost) shrine.

Then Carter drew back the doors of the fourth shrine.

A winged arm came into view. Carved into the stone of
a magnificent rose-tinted quartzite sarcophagus, the arm
stretched toward them. Carter recognized it as belonging
to the goddess Nephthys. She had been placed there, along
with three other goddesses, to protect the king against

This photo of the sarcophagus taken from above shows its
cracked lid.

intruders. From what Carter could see, the sarcophagus seemed to be in beautiful condition. When he rapped the sides of it with his knuckles, it rang like a bell.

It took six more weeks to remove the other delicate shrines. At last, only the sarcophagus remained in the burial chamber.

And Carter got his first good look at it. Its body was, indeed, a masterpiece. But the lid left him mystified. It was a huge, ill-fitting stone slab weighing more than one and a quarter tons. Made of cheaper granite, it had been tinted to match the rest of the sarcophagus, and a crack ran across its center. Obviously, it had broken in two in ancient times, then been carefully cemented and painted over. Had the original lid not been ready in time for the king's burial? Had this substitute one been dropped during his funeral? So many questions sprang to Carter's mind. But the most important one was this: What would he find beneath the lid?

He would soon find out.

While Carter focused on the sarcophagus and coffins, the political sandstorm roared toward him. The January elections had swept out of office those sympathetic to the British government. A new regime, under the Nationalists, took their place. Almost immediately, the new government appointed Morcos Bey Hanna to oversee the country's public works, including all historic sites. Morcos Bey knew practically nothing about archaeology, and he didn't care that much about Tutankhamun or the tomb. He did, however, detest foreigners, particularly the British, and he was sympathetic to any scheme that might force Carter out of the tomb, the Valley, and Egypt itself. So when the new minister met Lacau, he recognized an ally. Morcos Bey wanted the British to leave. Lacau wanted the antiquities to stay. Together, they were about to make life difficult for Howard Carter.

On February 12, 1924, Carter held another ceremony in the tomb. As the invited guests, including Pierre Lacau, crowded into the burial chamber, they fell silent. "Past and present seemed to meet," said Carter.

The spectators took their seats, and Carter glanced at the complicated tackle that had been set up to raise the heavy lid. It looked to be in working order. Already, Harry Burton's motion picture camera had begun to whir as the workmen put their shoulders to the tackle's ropes.

Carter gave the signal. The chain hoists clanked and the ropes grew taut. The lid trembled. Inch by inch it rose,

Lifting the heavy granite lid from the sarcophagus revealed Tutankhamun's outermost, gilt coffin. The coffin and sarcophagus would remain untouched just like this for almost a year as Carter and Egyptian officials wrangled over several issues.

until it swung in midair two feet above the sarcophagus. Then the men secured the tackle ropes, and Carter stepped forward with his flashlight.

Light shone into the sarcophagus for the first time in more than three thousand years. For a moment, cold disappointment shot through Carter. He saw nothing . . . nothing but discolored funeral palls that covered the contents like a blanket. Fingers trembling, he rolled back the shrouds one by one. Sections of the brittle linens crumbled at his touch. His heart pounded. Sweat stained his white shirt. At last he removed the final shroud and "a gasp of wonderment escaped our lips, so gorgeous was the sight that met our eyes," he recalled.

A magnificent golden figure filled the sarcophagus. It was a man-shaped coffin—an effigy of the boy king—seven feet long and made of wood covered in gold. The hands, crossed over the chest, held the royal emblems—the crook and the flail—made of gold and faience. On its forehead the twin heads of a sacred cobra, important symbols of a pharaoh's power, appeared poised to strike.

Carter noted a tiny wreath of cornflowers and olive leaves resting on the coffin's forehead. They still had a tinge of blue. He thought there was nothing as beautiful as those few withered flowers left behind by a loved one.

Gazing at them, he could almost hear the ghostly foot-steps of the king's departing mourners.

Minutes later, he escorted his guests back up the stairs, where they blinked in the blazing sunlight and breathed deeply of the fresh air. But Carter's thoughts lingered on the splendor of that vanished pharaoh. And the words, inscribed on his coffin, felt carved on his heart: "Oh, Mother Nut! Spread thy wings over me as the Imperishable Stars."

The next morning, Carter prepared for another group of visitors—the wives of the excavation team. But instead a messenger rode up to Carter's house with a letter from Pierre Lacau.

His words hit Carter like a thunderclap. Lacau for-bade the wives' visit! "The ministry [under the direction of Morcos Bey Hanna]," wrote the director, "does not permit the admission of [them] into the tomb."

Carter seethed. How dare Lacau and Morcos Bey try to tell *him* whom he could or could not invite into the tomb! It was an insult too far. In a fury, he rode to the excava-tion site and told the team what had happened. They, too, were insulted. If their wives could not be given the com-mon courtesy of seeing what they'd been working on for the past fifteen months, then they would stop work.

Storming into the tomb, Carter cut the power lines, then slammed shut the thick steel door and padlocked it. Dropping the only set of keys into the pocket of his tweed jacket, he headed into Luxor.

He left the heavy granite lid as it was—swinging several feet above the golden coffin and held in place by nothing more than a makeshift series of hoists and pulleys. Surely *this* would cause Lacau and Morcos Bey to back down. Tons of stone suspended over priceless artifacts? Carter felt confident the new government would quickly apologize for its insult.

In Luxor, he posted a notice on the Winter Palace's bulletin board. He knew that the wealthiest, most politically connected people in Egypt would eventually walk through that lobby. He wanted them all to know what had happened. He wrote: "Owing to impossible restrictions and discourtesies on the part of the Public Works Department and its antiquities service, all my collaborators, in protest, have refused to work any further upon the scientific investigations of the discoveries of the tomb of Tutankhamun."

His actions enraged Lacau. He demanded Carter turn over the keys.

Carter refused.

So Lacau sent an ultimatum: Return to work in forty-eight hours or face cancellation of the concession.

Again, Carter refused.

And Lacau did as he'd threatened. He took away the concession. The Egyptian government, he declared, was free to continue the work itself.

A week later, at Carter's urging, Reis Ahmed Gerigar went to check on the tomb. Suddenly, a column of police on camels and donkeys thundered toward him across the Valley floor. At their head rode Director Lacau. When the men reached the tomb, Lacau dismounted. He announced to Gerigar that the government was officially taking control of the tomb.

Standing his ground, Gerigar blocked the tomb's entrance.

But Lacau ordered him to move aside.

Gerigar had no other choice. He stepped away.

Two locksmiths with hacksaws managed to cut through the padlock on the steel door. Because the electricity was still off, the men descended by candlelight into the tomb. To Lacau's relief, the heavy lid still hung in midair. It had not, as he'd feared, come crashing down on the delicate gold coffin. Carefully, the men swung the lid aside and lowered it to the floor. The contents of the sarcophagus had been saved.

And Morcos Bey and Lacau had made their point: The Egyptian people were the rightful owners of the tomb. To drive home this point, after a gala reopening ceremony on March 6, 1924, they threw open the tomb to Egyptian citizens. Over the next ten days, more than two thousand people shuffled down the rock-cut stairs and through the still treasure-filled chambers.

Carter, who'd gone to consult with lawyers in Cairo, shuddered when he heard about this. What archaeological evidence might those hordes be trampling and destroying? Were they picking up objects? Pocketing them? The situation plunged him into deep depression.

Locked out of the tomb, and unsure of what to do next, he reluctantly accepted a lucrative offer to speak about the discovery to audiences across the United States. Everywhere he spoke—New York; Chicago; Washington, DC—he fascinated audiences. But his heart wasn't in it. Instead, he brooded in hotel rooms and declined invitations to parties and dinners. He was coming to the sickening realization that he would never work in his beloved Valley again. He would never get the chance to look upon the face of Tutankhamun's mummy.

When his tour in the United States ended in June, Carter sailed for England, a lonely and defeated man.

It was said . . . an ancient god from the afterlife watched the tomb.

In those blistering summer months of 1924, few people came to the Valley of the Kings. It was too hot. Besides, the biggest tourist attraction—Tutankhamun's tomb—was closed for the season. From the Valley's lonely cliffs, Reis Ahmed Gerigar and a handful of workers kept an eye on the closed excavation site.

They did not trust the government's guards, or the Antiquities Service. And so they watched.

Something *else* appeared to be watching, too.

A jet-black jackal.

It lay on the slope opposite the tomb. Ears alert. Eyes trained. Still as stone.

Odd, noted the workers. Who had ever seen a *black* jackal? Black jackals no longer lived in Egypt.

Odder still, it looked very much like the creature pictured on the burial chamber's wall: Anubis, the god of death and the afterlife, of burial rites and mummification.

Anubis, the half *jackal*.

The superstitious among the men claimed powerful magic was at work. They insisted the animal *was* Anubis, come to watch over the king's mummy. For now, they said, the god was quiet. But what would he do if the excavation resumed? What would happen if the pharaoh's coffins were opened?

CHAPTER 11

The Mummy Unwrapped
JANUARY–NOVEMBER 1925

For nearly a year, the tomb sat untouched. Sand drifted over the stone-cut stairs. Silence settled over its chambers.

In Cairo, the various parties involved in its excavation argued and wrangled and went to court. All sides knew that they had to work things out. Carter couldn't continue his work without permission from the Antiquities Service. And the Antiquities Service now realized that there was no archaeologist better able to do the job than Carter. They needed him to come back.

It helped Carter's cause that Morcos Bey Hanna had been thrown out of office. So had many other members of the Nationalist Party. That's because on November 19, 1924, the British government finally found an excuse to reinstate its full authority in Egypt. That day, a terrorist had shot Sir Lee Stack, the British commander of the Egyptian Army. The British moved quickly. Troops moved in and seized control of the country. Nationalists were removed from office and replaced by pro-British men. These new officeholders were eager to come to an arrangement as soon as possible. Since the tomb's takeover, no work of any kind had been carried out. And Lacau, who remained as director of the Antiquities Service, was deeply concerned for the safety of those thousands of treasures still in the chambers.

At last, the parties came to an agreement. Lady Carnarvon gave up any claim to the tomb. She also canceled her husband's contract giving the London *Times* first news. In return, the Egyptian government promised to repay what her husband had spent on finding and excavating the tomb. As for Carter, the Antiquities Service offered to hire him as head archaeologist on the project. If he accepted, he'd now be working *for* Lacau. The director, however, promised not to interfere with his work.

It was enough for Carter. After accepting the offer, he rushed back to Egypt and headed straight for the excavation site.

Were all the artifacts still there? Were they in good shape?

Descending into the tomb, he checked each chamber. He was relieved to see that everything was in order except for a few missing tools.

But at the front of the laboratory tomb, Carter found a sad sight. The beautiful, rosette-sprinkled shroud that had hung over the second shrine for thousands of years had been left on the ground outside the lab's entrance. "It is ruined!" moaned Carter.

He spent the rest of the season in the laboratory, conserving the items that had been taken from the tomb the year before. He packed off nineteen more crates of artifacts to the museum in Cairo before returning to London for the summer. But he would be back in the fall to open Tutankhamun's coffins. Would he find the king's mummy inside?

On October 13, 1925, Carter and his team gathered around the open sarcophagus. Using a pulley, the workers slowly hoisted the lid of the outer coffin to reveal a second coffin similar to the first. This one, too, was made of wood and covered with beaten gold. And like the outer coffin, it showed the image of a king. But this second coffin was more magnificent than the first. Its thick gold foil was entirely encrusted with richly colored cut glass—red, blue, and turquoise.

Carter's system of hoists and rigging lifts the second coffin from the outermost one.

Carter longed to pull off the lid of this second coffin and see what lay inside. But he controlled himself. Before they could go any further, the outer coffin and its contents had to be lifted from the sarcophagus.

It was a harder job than anyone expected. Straining, the men pulled on the ropes with all their strength. What could be making it so heavy? With great effort they lifted the coffins, slid wooden planks underneath the load, and laid it on top of the sarcophagus.

Carter bent over the second coffin for a closer look. It fit so tightly into the outer one that he couldn't slide his little finger between them. How to lift it? All he could do was ease out . . . just a quarter of an inch . . . some bronze pins that held down the second coffin's lid. Sweat dripped from his brow as he tied some wire around the pins. Would it hold? Carter and the team were about to find out. Using the wire, he hoisted the coffin into mid-air. It swung there precariously as Carter and the workers returned the outer shell to the sarcophagus. Then carefully . . . so carefully . . . inch by inch . . . the second coffin was lowered back onto the planks.

Carter, whose nerves had been, he admitted, "at an almost painful tension," breathed a sigh of relief.

When the men removed the lid of the second coffin, they saw that a red linen shroud had been carefully tucked around a third coffin. Only the burnished gold face of the coffin remained uncovered. With trembling hands, Carter rolled back the shroud. He blinked in astonishment.

The third coffin was made of solid gold!

"How great must have been the wealth buried with those ancient Pharaohs?" Carter thought at that moment. "What riches that valley must have once concealed!" Tutankhamun was probably the *least* important of the twenty-seven kings buried there. Imagine the treasures

The third coffin covered with a linen shroud as it lay in the shell of the second coffin.

that must have been left in the other tombs. No wonder ancient robbers found them irresistible.

And no wonder the load had been so heavy.

Solid gold!

Carter bent over the third coffin. The most richly decorated of all, it was inlaid with semiprecious stones. Exquisite winged goddesses decorated it, their arms outstretched to encircle the king's body protectively.

But . . . what was this? The archaeologist touched his finger to a thick black coating that covered much of the coffin.

During Tutankhamun's funeral, priests had poured buckets of a tar-like substance over most of the coffin. Through the centuries, the stuff had congealed into a thick mass. Not only did it cover most of the third coffin, but it also worked like superglue, leaving the third coffin stuck fast inside the second one.

Struggling under its weight, workmen moved the third coffin, still stuck inside the shell of the second, into the Antechamber. Since the artifacts in this room had already been removed, the scientists had more space in which to work.

Alfred Lucas, the chemist, knelt beside the coffin and scraped off a bit of the black substance. It was soft and a little rubbery. Naturally, he would need to do some scientific tests to figure out how to remove the stuff. But why wait for his results? They could take days. Why not go ahead and lift the lid of the third coffin?

Eagerly, Carter and three other members of the team grasped the lid's golden handles. For a moment, the lid stuck. Then they raised it and saw—

The mummy!

It was neatly wrapped in linen bandages held in place by decorated gold bands. A pair of golden hands, sewn to the wrappings, held a crook and flail. And across its

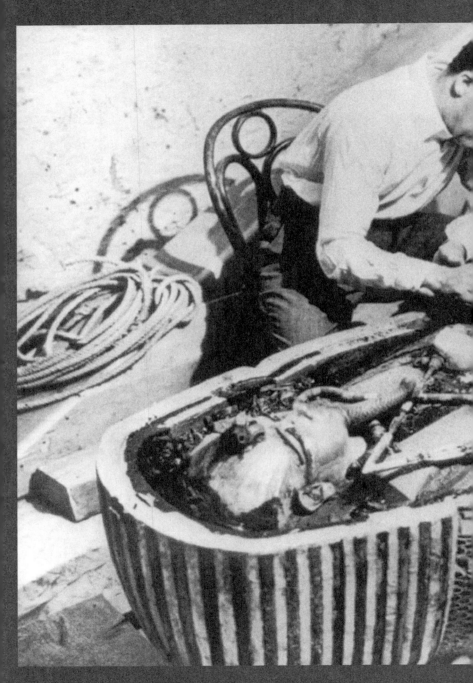

Carter and an unknown reis gaze at the innermost coffin still stuck inside the second one, October 1925. Notice the black tar-like substance on and around it.

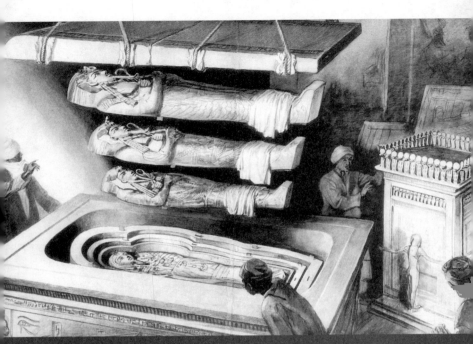

A 1925 drawing from a German magazine diagrams for its readers how Tutankhamun's coffins nestled together and fit inside the sarcophagus. The outermost (first coffin) was made of wood covered with a thin layer of beaten gold. The second wooden coffin was also covered with beaten gold and inlaid with brilliantly colored glass. The third coffin was made of solid gold, inside which lay the mummy, decorated with gold bands, a gold mask, and hands of sheet gold. Obviously, the artist of this diagram did not visit the tomb; otherwise he wouldn't have included the shrine containing the king's canopic jars in the illustration (which was in the Treasury, not the burial chamber). Additionally, the mummy shown resting inside the third coffin looks nothing like the actual one.

chest lay a large golden bird, its wings spread wide as if in flight. The ancient Egyptians believed that at death the spirit flew free, but that it returned to the body when it was ready to enjoy eternal life. This is why they took such care in mummifying the body. It needed to be perfectly preserved so the spirit would recognize it when it returned to the tomb.

Most astonishing of all, the mummy wore a helmet-like golden mask, made in the king's image and covering its entire head and shoulders. Ancient Egyptians called it

A close-up of the mummy's torso shows both the golden hands and the bird spread across Tutankhamun's chest.

the "head of mystery." They believed it allowed the king to see in the afterlife and drive away anything that might attack him. Wearing it was described as "seeing with the head of a god."

The mask had eyes made of obsidian, and its eyelids were lined with blue glass. Adorned with a blue ceremonial beard, it was surrounded by a blue-and-gold-striped headdress. A vulture and cobra on the forehead of the headdress looked ready to spit at the king's enemies.

Thirty-two hundred years had passed since anyone had looked down into the deep, dark eyes of the boy pharaoh. Now, as Carter gazed at the mask, he was so moved he couldn't speak. The youth's expression looked sad and gentle. It was, Carter thought, the face of one who had not expected to die so soon.

Unfortunately, the same tar-like substance that covered the coffin had been poured over both the mummy and the mask. The stuff was like superglue. Carter could not remove the mask from the mummy, or lift the mummy from the coffin. What to do?

For the next few days, he waited impatiently as Alfred Lucas experimented with the black substance. But no matter what the frustrated chemist tried, nothing dissolved it. At last, he discovered that the stuff melted with heat. And

The king's gold mask coated with tar-like unguents and looking as it did when Carter and others first saw it.

so workmen carried the two glued-together coffins containing the mummy out of the tomb. They left it beneath the blazing sun.

It lay there for hours. Its temperature soared. But even after reaching a roasting 149 degrees Fahrenheit, the glue didn't soften. Not one little bit. Carter resigned himself. He would just have to examine the mummy in its coffins.

They took a group photo first—Carter and Lacau, along with various Egyptian and European guests. Posed around the coffins in the dark, narrow entrance of the laboratory tomb, the men smiled for the camera. It was, after all, a momentous day. November 11, 1925, a day to commemorate. The day of the mummy's unwrapping.

No one present seemed to care that removing the mummy's bandages meant permanently destroying it. No one seemed concerned that rifling through the boy king's human remains was indecent or a sacrilege. Even Carter, who took great care in conserving the tomb's objects, saw no reason why the mummy shouldn't be unwrapped. And Director Lacau, whose job it was to *preserve* Egypt's ancient artifacts—mummies included—did nothing to stop the unwrapping, either. Indeed, he had insisted on observing—even enjoying—the event.

Only Dr. Douglas Derry, the anatomist from Cairo University, looked solemn. And no wonder. He'd been given the job of cutting open the bandages. One wrong move and the only chance in history to study an intact royal mummy would be ruined.

Photograph taken, Derry got down to work. From his medical bag he pulled a blue school exercise book. In pencil, he neatly filled out the blanks on the book's front cover:

NAME: Tut Ankh Amon

CLASS: Royal

SUBJECT: Anatomy

SCHOOL: 1356 BC–1925 AD

Kneeling beside the coffins, sweat dripping off his face, Derry took a deep breath. Then he plunged his scalpel into the mummy's chest just below the golden face mask. He sliced through stiffened bandages, all the way down to its toes. Then he peeled back the two flaps he'd made.

Gold!

On the left side of the body lay a golden band decorated with the wiggling body of a sacred cobra. A paper-thin golden pectoral, or breastplate, surrounded the king's throat. In the second layer, they found a pure gold knife intricately decorated with scenes of a hunt. Carter thought it must have been one of the king's most prized possessions.

THE CURSE OF THE MUMMY

Unfortunately, the wrappings themselves were in bad shape. Resembling crumbly black charcoal, they turned to ash when touched. Carter blamed the black substance that had been poured over the body for the damage. Others wondered if the mummy's time in the sun had been the cause.

After making a few notes in his exercise book, Derry took up his scalpel again and began cutting away the

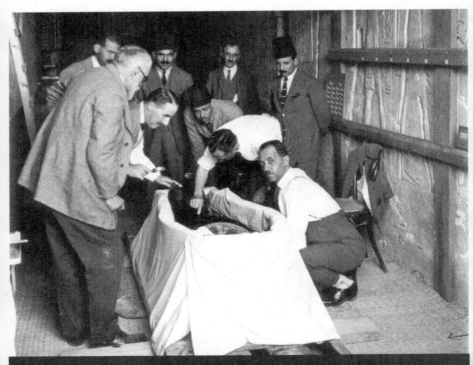

The king's autopsy. From left to right: Director Pierre Lacau, Howard Carter brandishing his magnifying glass, Dr. Douglas Derry bending over the mummy, perhaps about to make the first cut, and Dr. Saleh Bey Hamdi kneeling and facing the photographer. Assorted guests and VIPs crowd into the background.

linens around the mummy's feet. Carter knelt beside him, peering through his magnifying glass with delight.

Unlike previously discovered mummies, stripped of all jewelry by ancient robbers, Tutankhamun's was covered in precious items. Each of these ornaments had been precisely placed on the body by ancient priests. As they had, they'd muttered magic spells. These spells, they'd believed, gave each item a special power. While Carter did not know the purpose of all the ornaments, he understood they'd been put there for the help and guidance of the dead king. As he knelt beside the mummy, he realized just how much ancient Egyptians had feared the dangers of the underworld. He also recognized the love, care, and respect that had gone into Tutankhamun's burial.

This thought, however, did not keep the men from pulling apart the mummy's wrappings. Neither Carter nor Derry stopped to consider that they were dealing with the remains of a real human being. Neither saw their actions as a sacrilege even though preparing Tutankhamun's body for the afterlife had been a deeply religious act that held great meaning for ancient Egyptians. The preserved body of the king was never meant to be seen, and yet here were scientists, rummaging through its wrappings, trying to discover everything—even the most sacred of secrets.

Again and again, objects came into view.

Again and again, Derry stopped work so each item could be carefully labeled, recorded, and photographed before being touched.

The slow, meticulous work bored the guests. One by one they wandered out of the laboratory tomb. By the time the sun dipped behind the Theban hills, even Director Lacau had gone home.

For the next five days, Derry and Carter moved through layers of linen. Beneath the bandages wrapped around the feet they found that Tutankhamun wore gold sandals. Hidden in the bandages covering his arms lay a treasury of bracelets—thirteen in all. On his chest rested a profusion of golden collars, amulets, and scarabs made of lapis lazuli. Probing even deeper, Carter uncovered a breathtaking gold hawk-shaped pectoral, inlaid with hundreds of glass pieces. A layer below that, he came across another massive pectoral portraying the vulture goddess, Nekhbet. It was, Carter believed, one of the most beautiful pieces of jewelry ever created. In all, he and Derry found 143 glorious items as they pawed through the mummy's thirteen layers of wrapping.

Finally, Tutankhamun's body—with the exception of the gold mask that remained glued to his head—lay bare

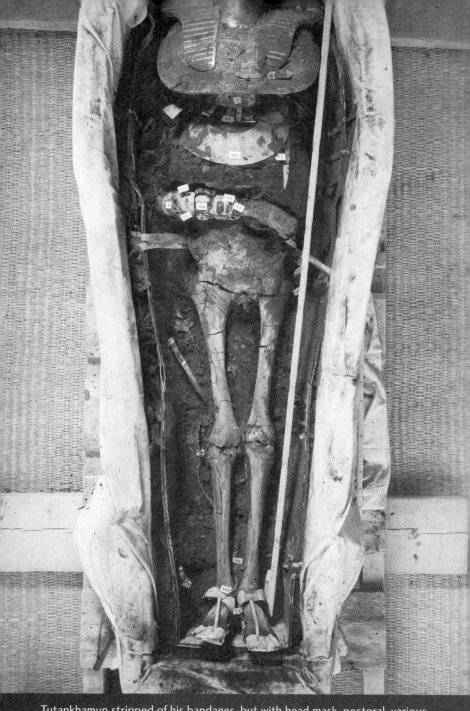

Tutankhamun stripped of his bandages, but with head mask, pectoral, various amulets, and golden sandals still on his body.

before them. Its gray flesh—brittle and cracking—had shrunk, leaving little more than skin and bones. Carter could see the place where the ancient embalmers had made their incision on the left side of the stomach to remove all the king's precious organs.

Derry bent to take measurements. But when he touched one of the mummy's legs, some of the withered flesh flaked away down to the bone. So Derry, with the

Tutankhamun's body, looking small and delicate, after being stripped of all linen wrappings and ornaments.

help of Dr. Saleh Bey Hamdi, an anatomist from Cairo University, painted the whole thing with melted paraffin wax to keep it from crumbling any further.

This action seems wasted, considering what the men did next.

Since the mummy was still glued to the bottom of the coffin, the team could not remove all the jewelry. So they cut off its arms in order to slide off the bracelets. They cut the torso in half, too, and sawed off the head, before using a chisel and hammer to gouge out each body piece. Derry and Hamdi examined each piece. From the ends of various bones, they estimated that Tutankhamun had died at around the age of eighteen.

The coffin was now empty except for Tutankhamun's head and neck still stuck inside the gold mask. Obviously, the men couldn't take a chisel and hammer to this priceless artifact. Instead, the two doctors separated the head from the mask by sliding heated knives between them. With a soft sucking sound, the mask pulled away.

Beneath a few more layers of bandages, a gold-and-carnelian crown glistened on the king's head. Down through a few more layers, Derry discovered a golden band, and farther down still, fitted over the king's shaved head, a skullcap made of linen and decorated with thousands of

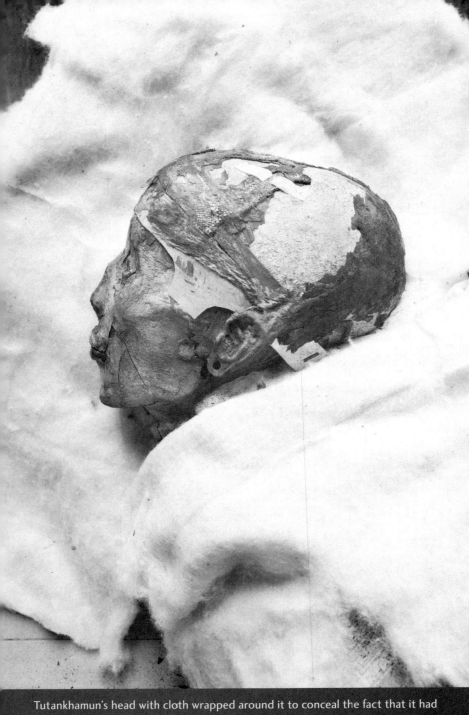

Tutankhamun's head with cloth wrapped around it to conceal the fact that it had been severed from the king's body.

tiny gold and faience beads. This was the one ornament Carter chose not to remove. Too fragile, it was painted with a thin coating of wax and left in place.

At last, at the touch of Derry's sable brush, the final fragments of decayed linen fell away, and . . .

Carter came face-to-face with Tutankhamun. The teenager, wrote Carter, was "refined and cultured, the features well-formed, especially the clearly marked lips." The men noted the long eyelashes, the slightly protruding front teeth and pierced ears. They noted something else, too. On the mummy's left cheek was a round scab that had yet to heal.

What was it? Some kind of wound?

Neither Dr. Derry nor Dr. Hamdi knew.

Much to Carter's disappointment, they couldn't come up with any clues as to why the pharaoh had died so young, either. There didn't seem to be any evidence of disease. Could he have had an accident . . . or maybe even been murdered? It was all speculation.

Alfred Lucas, however, had figured out *when* the boy died. The flowers found in the tomb only bloomed in March or April. Assuming Tutankhamun had spent the usual seventy days in the embalming house (the time it

One of twenty views of the gold mask, cleaned and conserved, taken by photographer Harry Burton. The mask has become an iconic symbol of Egypt.

took to embalm a pharaoh), he must have died in late January or early February. And that meant the king's funeral happened in early spring . . . the same time of year as Lord Carnarvon's.

An unnamed Egyptian boy wearing a necklace and pectoral from Tutankhamun's mummy. Some people claim this is the same boy who found the first stair leading to the tomb five years earlier, but that has not been confirmed.

It was said . . . the mark on the mummy's cheek was a mosquito bite . . . and identical to Lord Carnarvon's.

Some people took this as proof of the curse. The vengeful pharaoh, they claimed, had killed Lord Carnarvon in the same way he himself had died. Surely, it could not be coincidental that both men had mosquito bites in the exact same place.

But was Tutankhamun's mark in the very same location as Carnarvon's?

Doctors could not confirm this.

Still, believers didn't need confirmation. They knew the curse had been awakened.

Who would be its next victim?

CHAPTER 12

Fabulous Finds

OCTOBER 1926–APRIL 1927

The fifth season started in the laboratory. Carter, with the help of Alfred Lucas, carefully arranged the mummy pieces in a tray of sand so that it looked intact. They folded the arms across the chest and covered it in wads of cotton wool. Then they placed the entire tray in the outermost coffin. Solemnly, and with no ceremony, a handful of workmen carried the coffin into the tomb and placed it back inside the sarcophagus. Carter, who often found himself awed and deeply moved by such moments, seemed unbothered by the king's reburial. "The King's mummy . . . was lowered into the sarcophagus this morning," he matter-of-factly wrote in his journal on October 23, 1926. "We are now ready to begin upon the investigation of the [Treasury]."

The boards he'd put up three years earlier to keep himself from being distracted by the chamber's glittering contents were now yanked away.

Carter jumped.

The statue of a black jackal sitting just inside the doorway had startled him. The dog lay on its tummy with its face forward and its paws out flat in front. It had a long muzzle and large, pointed ears. With its long, fluid lines it looked hyperalert, ready to spring at the tomb's intruders.

This was Anubis, and as the major god of the dead and embalming, it was his job to watch over and guard the deceased king. Anubis also served as an important symbol of death and the transition to the afterlife. Some myths even credited him with being the inventor of mummification. It was believed that Anubis oversaw the embalming process.

The statue fascinated Carter. Had the features of this god been inspired by those of the real jackals who roamed the desert? He doubted it. The jackals hanging around the Valley were smaller and brown. Black jackals, if they had ever roamed the Egyptian desert, were no longer seen.

Once workmen carried the jackal statue from the tomb, Carter and the team investigated the rest of the Treasury. There were scores of human figures made of

Statue of the god Anubis on its pylon. Behind it can be seen the golden canopic shrine and the solid gold head of the cow goddess, Hathor.

clay and wood called ushabti. Ushabti, also known as "the answerers," were the slaves, servants, and soldiers who would magically come to life and do the king's bidding in the afterlife. Additionally, there was a fleet of model boats, the piled-up pieces of two hunting chariots, and a row of treasure chests decorated with ebony, ivory, and gold. These contained jewels and other treasures, like an exquisite ostrich-feather fan with an ivory handle.

A handful of painted wooden ushabti found in the Treasury and meant to do the king's bidding in the afterlife.

At the back of the room, almost touching the ceiling, was a gilt wood shrine. Inside, Carter discovered an alabaster chest divided into four compartments. Each compartment contained a pure gold, miniature casket. Carter carefully opened the coffins: One contained Tutankhamun's liver, wrapped in linen; another, his lungs; the third, his stomach; and the fourth, his intestines.

Carter hoped to find some personal writings in the Treasury. These would have been on papyrus, the thick paper made by ancient Egyptians from the stem of the papyrus plant. Anything that might throw a light on the times in which Tutankhamun lived would have been welcome— a series of letters, perhaps, or archives of some sort, even a family tree. What was the teenager like as a person and a ruler? Was his short reign an uneasy one? How had he died? But to Carter's disappointment, no papyrus rolls were found.

That left just the small room off the Antechamber that Carter called the Annex. Would he find writings there? Carter remembered the first time he'd peeked into the room. It had been during that thrilling night visit to the tomb. He'd crawled beneath a couch in the Antechamber and looked through a hole made in the doorway by the robbers. It had been a huge mess.

It still was. Though ancient priests had tidied up other parts of the tomb after the break-ins, when it came to the Annex, it didn't look as if they'd bothered. Bedsteads, chairs, footstools, game boards, baskets of dried fruit, every kind of alabaster vessel and pottery wine jars, boxes of funerary figures, toys, shields, bows and arrows, and more had been jumbled together by the thieves. All,

The floor of the Annex covered with artifacts strewn about by ancient robbers. On the white chest to the right can be seen the dirt footprints left behind by one of the thieves. Once again, Carter has numbered the objects.

remarked Carter, had been turned "topsy-turvy." Here was a broken box bulging with delicate faience cups. There was a sandal. An alabaster figure of a lion lay wedged beneath a casket of broken pottery. A crushed wooden cabinet spilled its contents of robes and gloves. Dozens of objects had been haphazardly piled up—in some places all the way to the ceiling—creating a wobbling tower of grave goods. There wasn't an inch of empty floor space.

Carter felt overwhelmed. He needed to clear away an area in which to work. But how? His solution was an uncomfortable one. Fitting a rope sling under his armpits, he dangled headfirst from the doorway. For hours, with sweat dripping from his face and the rope biting into his skin, he gently, *gently* eased out the first objects. Any sudden movement, he knew, could cause an avalanche of antiquities.

It took weeks, but Carter managed to clear some floor space. He soon recognized the chamber's purpose. It had been built as a storeroom for wine, oils, perfumes, and other practical items the king needed in his afterlife. He could also easily imagine robbers ransacking the place for loot. Inside some of the jars of sticky oil, he found finger marks where the contents had been scooped out. And on the lid of a white painted box he saw the bare footprints, dirty and black, of one of the thieves.

What he didn't find were papyrus rolls.

Not a single one.

Carter thus resigned himself to piecing together Tutankhamun's life by his grave goods. After all, every artifact had a story to tell. What did they suggest? The king's mummy, like his statues, showed him to be a slim youth with a large head. His painted chests and decorated

One of Carter's favorite artifacts—a long fan of wood covered with sheet gold (the ostrich feather is missing)—depicts the boy king bowhunting from his chariot as his dogs run alongside. Depictions like this one helped Carter decipher the mystery of Tutankhamun's short life.

chairs depicted him as an avid hunter, a dog lover, and an affectionate husband. In his mind, Carter saw the teen-aged ruler racing his slughi hounds across marsh and desert, and hunting ducks among the Nile reeds with his slender, smiling wife. But these were just glimmerings. The mystery of the king's life eluded him. "The shadows move," he said, "but the dark is never quite uplifted."

It was said . . . that Howard Carter saw Anubis.

It happened after another long day of restoring the artifacts removed from the Treasury. Home at last, Carter lingered on the veranda. He let his eyes settle on the hills behind his house. Some people might have found them stark and forbidding. But Carter thought they had a beauty all their own. He watched with pleasure as the shadows lengthened, changing from the soft lavender of twilight to the gray-blue of evening.

A movement caught his eye.

Two jackals picked their way down the slope. The first was of normal size and coloring. But the second . . .

Carter grabbed his binoculars for a closer look.

The second was tall, slender, and black as midnight. It looked exactly like the statue that had once stood in the Treasury doorway. The very statue that Carter—just that morning—had wrapped in cotton wool and packed into a crate.

In all his thirty-five years in Egypt, the archaeologist had never seen a jackal like this one.

The creature stopped and turned its head. It stared at Carter.

Carter stared back.

For a moment, for an eternity, their eyes locked.

Then the jackal loped away, disappearing into the shadows.

And Carter dropped into a chair. He had recognized the creature. It was, he confessed that night in his diary, "the old and original Egyptian known as . . . Anubis."

But what had the god of death wanted with him?

CHAPTER 13

Work Complete

FEBRUARY 1932

I t was done. After ten years and the removal of 5,398 items, the work in the tomb was complete. All that remained was to sweep out the chambers.

Carter did it himself. Alone, in the empty silence of the tomb, he pushed the broom over the rock-cut floors. Did his mind wander back to those thrilling moments of the discovery: finding the first step; the first candlelit glimpse of the Antechamber's crowded wonders; the surprise and delight of the golden coffins? He must have thought of Lord Carnarvon. How sad it was that he hadn't been there to share it all. He must have thought, too, about the many problems he'd had to tackle.

Clearing the tomb, he admitted, had been "a long and steady plod." There had been times over the years when he felt trapped by the very discovery that had left him speechless with wonder. For ten years he had descended those sixteen finely chiseled stairs to work in the stuffy chambers. He'd been a servant to Tutankhamun as surely as those who'd waited upon the king thirty-two hundred years earlier.

"I pitied [Carter] cooped up in the electrified darkness of the tomb," said one colleague.

"We can only say how lucky it is all in the hands of Carter," said another.

Never before had a tomb been cleared so carefully. Carter had given loving attention to every object, no matter how small or seemingly insignificant. He'd made detailed notes and accurate drawings of everything found. He'd had photographs taken, and had sought the help of the best available scientists. He'd refused to be hurried. "There is great danger in haste," he liked to say. Ultimately, he gave the world the invaluable gifts of knowledge, art, and beauty.

But it was all over now—the recording, the conserving, even the sweeping out. Still, Carter lingered. Stepping down into the burial chamber, he rested a hand on the sarcophagus. A large glass plate had been placed over it instead of its original lid. Carter looked down into the golden face of the outermost coffin. Where was Tutankhamun's spirit now? Had it made the journey to the underworld? Or was it soaring in the radiant Egyptian skies high above the Valley of the Kings?

It was time to go. Howard Carter climbed the steps of the tomb into the fresh air. Soon he would head to London to start writing a book about the tomb's excavation. But perhaps before he did, he took one last walk up the scree-covered slope to the eastern edge of the Theban Mountains to stand, once more, in his favorite spot.

It was said . . . that as Carter cleared the tomb, the curse took more revenge.

What else could have caused the death of Aubrey Herbert, Lord Carnarvon's half brother? He'd been present at the opening of the sarcophagus, but died just months later during what was rumored as a bout of insanity.

And what about Lady Elizabeth Carnarvon? While she had never visited the tomb, she *did* die of an insect bite, just like her brother Lord Carnarvon.

Or consider the case of Arthur Mace. As a member of the excavation team, he went in and out of the tomb constantly and handled numerous artifacts. In 1924, he began experiencing fatigue, shortness of breath, and indigestion. He became so ill that he had to give up his work in the Valley and retire to England. But his health did not improve. Weak and bedridden, he died four years later in 1928.

Curse believers chalked up all these deaths to the wrath of the pharaoh.

And there were other suspicious cases, too.

Take, for instance, the death of Dr. Aaron Ember. A noted Egyptologist at Johns Hopkins University, Ember had never visited the tomb. But he *was* a friend to many of those present at its opening. On the night of June 1, 1926, his house outside Baltimore, Maryland, burst into flames. He might have escaped had he not run back into the burning building to rescue a manuscript. Its rumored title? *The Egyptian Book of the Dead*. Ember, along with his wife, his son, and their maid, died in the fire. Was it the curse's doing?

And then there were the strange and mysterious events surrounding the death of Richard Bethell. As Lord Carnarvon's personal secretary, he had attended the opening of the boy king's burial chamber. Seven years later, in 1929, Bethell was found dead in his London bedroom. How? Why? Police were baffled. But those who believed in the curse weren't. They knew the cause of death.

Just three months later, Bethell's father, Lord Westbury, flung himself from the window of his seventh-story apartment. Newspaper reporters claimed that for months he'd been muttering "the curse of the pharaohs" over and over again. Supposedly, he even kept an artifact from Tutankhamun's tomb in his bedroom inscribed with the curse warning: "Death shall come on swift wings to him that toucheth the tomb of the king."

Some readers thought this last detail was just too coincidental to be true.

How, then, countered curse believers, did one explain Lord Westbury's suicide note? Its first sentence reportedly and ominously read: "I really cannot stand any more horrors."

But the horrors didn't end there. On the way to the cemetery, Lord Westbury's hearse ran over two boys. One of them, an eight-year-old, died.

Curse believers buzzed. Death really *did* come to those who had disturbed the peace of the pharaoh.

And sometimes it even came to those who hadn't.

CHAPTER 14

Exit Carter

JUNE 1932–MARCH 1939

Carter spent the next year writing about the discovery of the tomb.

And then?

And when he finished his account? He did practically nothing else.

In the summers, he went to London. But the rest of the year, he lived in his house on the hill near the Valley of the Kings. He rarely visited the tomb. Instead, dressed in a three-piece suit, he sat on the veranda of the Winter Palace, eager to tell the story of his great discovery to anyone willing to listen. When people asked him what he was going to do next, he said he planned on searching for Alexander the Great's tomb. He claimed he knew exactly where it was. But he never told anyone its location.

Howard Carter looking confident, successful, and definitely not dressed for excavation.

He never excavated again. Instead, Carter lived quietly. He had few guests and fewer invitations. And he didn't seek out the company of his fellow Egyptologists. No matter his accomplishments, he still felt like an outsider. His colleagues, he believed, still looked down on him for not being a "gentleman."

And he was right. Despite his extraordinary discovery, not a single British institution recognized him. He received no honorary college degrees or admittance into prestigious science societies. He was offered no special teaching positions. He was given no awards. His colleagues viewed him as nothing more than a man of practical abilities. He wasn't a *trained* Egyptologist, so how could he possibly be worthy of accolades from Britain's academics and scholars? No, Howard Carter simply wasn't one of them. In their eyes, he remained still lower class.

Yet that didn't explain why Carter gave up his life's work. It was as if his time in the tomb had drained him of enthusiasm and purpose. Said one Egyptologist, "In many ways the discovery of Tutankhamun's tomb was Carter's own 'curse' as he was unable to move on."

What most people didn't know was that Carter was seriously ill. Diagnosed with cancer, his health quickly deteriorated. He grew less and less active, and lost interest in most things. Eventually, he even gave up his Egyptian home and returned to London full-time to be close to his doctors. But no medical treatment could save him. On March 2, 1939, Howard Carter died.

Just five people braved the rain and cold to bury him. And only one of them, Lady Evelyn, had any connection to the discovery of the tomb. The rest of his professional colleagues stayed away. They didn't even send flowers.

It was a short, simple funeral service. There were no gilt shrines or golden coffins for Howard Carter. No lengthy burial ritual with spells and incantations. There were just a few words from the vicar and a plain gray headstone that read:

Howard Carter
Archaeologist and Egyptologist
1874–1939

It was said . . . the curse continued on its vengeful path.

In 1939, the delicate silver trumpet found in the burial chamber and supposedly used by King Tutankhamun to call his troops to battle was played on a radio broadcast. It was the first time it had sounded in more than three thousand years. Months later, World War II broke out.

Coincidence, or the curse?

In 1966, Egypt's director-general of antiquities, Mohammad Ibraham, agreed to send some of the tomb's artifacts to Paris for an exhibition. The day he made this decision public, a car struck and killed him.

Coincidence, or the curse?

In 1967, the silver trumpet from Tutankhamun's burial chamber was again played. Not long afterward, the Six-Day War between Egypt and Israel erupted.

Coincidence, or the curse?

In 1969, the last survivor of the excavation—Richard Adamson—claimed in an interview on British television that he didn't believe in the mummy's curse. Then he left the TV station and climbed into a cab. But on the way home, the cab suddenly swerved to avoid crashing into a truck. Adamson was flung from the car. He woke up in the hospital with multiple broken bones.

Coincidence, or the curse?

In 1972, the new director-general of antiquities, Gamal Mehrez, packed up some of the tomb's most breathtaking treasures for a multicity world tour that would take them out of Egypt for the next nine years. After crating the boy king's golden mask, Mehrez dropped dead of a heart attack.

Coincidence, or the curse?

That same year, the treasures headed to London. But the flight crew who transported them soon had bad luck. One got divorced. Another had a heart attack. And a third kicked the crate containing the gold mask and joked, "Look, I'm kicking the most expensive thing in the world." Not long afterward, he broke the same leg.

Coincidence, or the curse?

In 1990, the silver trumpet from the tomb sounded for the third time. It was followed by the outbreak of the Gulf War.

Coincidence, or the curse?

In 1992, a production crew headed to the Valley of the Kings to film a five-part television series about Carter's excavation. During the taping, the lights in Tutankhamun's tomb constantly flickered on and off. The director became ill with gallstones. The main cable holding up the elevator in the crew's hotel suddenly snapped, plunging two crew members twenty-one floors before finally coming to a stop. The presenter stopped breathing for several seconds one day. He claimed his vocal cords suddenly felt as if they had sandpaper lids on them. And the entire crew got pink eye.

Coincidence, or the curse?

In 2011, the silver trumpet from the tomb was sounded for the fourth time. That same year, the Egyptian Revolution erupted.

Coincidence, or the curse?

CHAPTER 15

Space Travelers, Poison, and Murderous Mold

A vengeful spirit from the underworld?

By the middle of the twentieth century, this idea seemed silly and old-fashioned. Few people believed in spiritualism anymore. The spirit curse gave way to another possibility: Could the ancient Egyptians have had sophisticated technology? Had knowledge of this technology been lost in the mists of time?

Author Erich von Däniken thought so. In his 1968 book, *Chariots of the Gods*, he argued that space travelers had visited the earth thousands of years ago. With high-tech antigravity devices they'd built the pyramids and introduced all sorts of modern marvels like lightbulbs and advanced mathematics. Von Däniken even claimed these extraterrestrial beings had taught the Egyptians the art of mummification and tomb building. Not for religious reasons, though. Instead, all this preparation was made because the space travelers had promised to reawaken them upon their return to earth. And then? The aliens would whisk the pharaohs (and their tomb goods) off in a spaceship to a new life somewhere in the cosmos. *This* was the real reason it was so important to protect the tombs. And so, the space travelers had shown the pharaohs how to build burial chambers in ways that made intruders sick or confused. To make extra sure, high-powered lasers had been trained on the tombs from outer space.

High-powered lasers?

Some people believed this explained why Lord Carnarvon and others had died after spending time in the tomb.

But why hadn't everyone died? How had Carter survived?

Although Von Däniken's theories were far-fetched and based on very little fact, he told a compelling story. Millions of readers worldwide bought his book. Many of them bought into his theories, too.

Forget spirit curses and spacemen, said archaeological writer Philipp Vandenberg. In his 1975 book, *The Curse of the Pharaohs*, he suggested other ways the Egyptians could have killed those who disturbed the tombs. Was it possible necropolis priests deliberately placed poison in the tombs? Maybe they'd drenched the mummy's bandages in cyanide made from peach pits, or laced tomb objects with scorpion venom. Maybe they'd soaked a candlewick in arsenic and lit it. In an airtight tomb, these deadly vapors would never have dissipated. Had poisonous candles been left to burn in Tutankhamun's burial chamber while tomb workers sealed the entrance? Any of these poisons would certainly have felled Lord Carnarvon.

Although archaeologists have found little or no evidence of poison placed in tombs, Dr. Zahi Hawass, a renowned Egyptologist, did recall a time when he entered a previously sealed tomb:

> *At that moment of discovery, I felt as though arrows of fire were attacking me. My eyes were closed and I could not breathe because of a bad smell. I looked into the room and discovered a very thick yellow powder around the . . . sarcophagus . . . I ran back out because of this smell. We bought masks for the workers who began to remove the material. I found out it was hematite, quarried near Baharia.*

Hematite, a common mineral used by the Egyptians for its red pigment, is not poisonous unless swallowed. So what had made the air in Dr. Hawass's tomb so toxic? In this case, more investigation is required. Still, most scientists think intentional poisoning as the cause of the curse is highly unlikely. After all, tombs would have had to remain free of poison so necropolis priests could go in and fix them after robberies or floods. Besides, if tombs really were full of poison, wouldn't archaeologists have found dead tomb robbers? Wouldn't most archaeologists themselves be dead?

Others have suggested that tomb builders lined the floors of underground burial chambers with radioactive uranium. And, indeed, the rocks in the Valley of the Kings do contain small amounts of naturally occurring uranium. In 2011, scientists measured the rocks to see how much radon—a radioactive gas given off when uranium decays—was present in twelve tombs in the Valley by checking the radon exposure of the guards who worked in these tombs. They discovered the guards received a radiation dose almost three times the United States safety limit. Could it be that Lord Carnarvon and others died of radiation poisoning? Is radiation really the cause of the curse?

Scientists are doubtful. They've found no archaeological evidence of this. Additionally, they find it hard to
believe that priests and tomb workers were familiar with
radioactivity or understood atomic decay.

Spirit curses, spacemen, and intentional poisoning? None
of this scientifically explained those curse-related deaths.
Still going on the assumption that Tutankhamun's tomb
really did contain something that killed, researchers began
taking a more empirical approach. They began looking for
accidental killers, such as histoplasmosis.

A fungus that grows on bat droppings, or guano, causes
histoplasmosis, an often deadly, pneumonia-like illness.
When the guano dries out, it produces a dust that can be
inhaled. Could Carnarvon have breathed in this fungus-
filled dust? Geoffrey Dean, a doctor in South Africa,
believed so, and published his theory in medical journals. In 1974, a professor of anatomy at the University of
Liverpool, Dr. R. G. Harrison, picked up on Dean's theory.
He asked the director of the Egyptian Antiquities Service if
bats had ever infested Tutankhamun's tomb. The director,
in turn, asked among the "old people who were present at
the time" the tomb was opened. They remembered that an

iron door made of bars was used for the first six months after the discovery. Every night, they claimed, bats had flown between the bars and filled the tomb. Every morning, Carter had to have them shooed out before beginning work. If this was truly the case, it might explain Carnarvon's death, as well as the deaths of others, especially Arthur Mace and George Jay Gould. But why hadn't Carter and other team members gotten sick? As experienced archaeologists, they'd come in frequent contact with bat guano at other sites over the years. This contact, it was believed, had made them immune to the disease.

But is histoplasmosis the most likely suspect? The theory, after all, is supported by nothing more than local memory. Carter himself never mentions the presence of bats in any of his writings about the tomb. Neither does anyone else on the archaeological team. Still, scientists continue to examine the possibility.

In 1993, an Italian doctor and amateur Egyptologist, Nicola Di Paolo, suggested another suspect: aspergillus. Aspergillus is a fungus that grows especially well on grain, and produces a poison called aflatoxin. Di Paolo suggested that the fungus might have been growing on the offerings of bread and raw grains stored in Tutankhamun's tomb. Could the poisonous spores of the fungus have been whisked around at the first gust of air when the long-sealed tomb was opened? Could Carnarvon have inhaled them? Some scientists insist it's possible.

Others, however, remain skeptical. Aspergillus needs damp conditions to grow. And while floodwater did seep into the tomb from time to time, when Carter entered it, it was desert dry. It doesn't seem possible to them that enough spores could have grown in this environment to kill people. Additionally, Carter himself had the chemist, Alfred Lucas, check the brown spots on the burial wall for mold. Lucas concluded they were long dead. Said F. DeWolfe Miller, a professor of epidemiology at the University of Hawaii at Manoa, "The idea that an underground tomb, after 3,000 years, would have some kind of bizarre microorganism in it that's going to kill somebody six weeks later and make it look exactly like [blood poisoning] is very hard to believe." He added that he didn't know a single archaeologist or tourist who'd ever experienced an illness due to tomb toxins. Still, mold-related explanations for the curse continue to be examined by scientists.

As do other possibilities such as rodent droppings, hookworms, and even anthrax. So far, scientists have found nothing conclusive.

*   *   *

Spirit curses, spacemen, intentional poisoning, and murderous molds? Maybe, just maybe, say some scientists, all those deaths were simply coincidental.

In 2002, Mark Nelson, an Australian scientist, carried out a study to prove or disprove the existence of the mummy's curse.

First, he listed all the people that Carter had recorded in his writings as being present for:

1. the breaking of the seals and the opening of the third door in February 1923

2. the opening of the sarcophagus in February 1924

3. the opening of the coffins in October 1925

4. the examination of the mummy in November 1925.

If a curse existed, Nelson reasoned, these twenty-five people would have had the most exposure to it. (Note: Nelson only used Westerners in his study, since the life expectancy of Egyptians at that time would have differed from that of Westerners.)

Next, he listed all the people recorded in Carter's writings as being in Egypt at the time, but *not* present at the tomb during the four events. He reasoned that this group had *not* been exposed to the so-called curse.

Then he gathered the dates of births and deaths for both lists of people (forty-four in all) and calculated how long each had lived.

He analyzed the data.

The results?

The average age of death for people exposed to the so-called curse was seventy years, and the average length of time between exposure to it and death was between thirteen and fifteen years. In the second, unexposed group, the average age of death was only five years longer—seventy-five.

Nelson concluded that no evidence of a mummy's curse existed. "Perhaps finally it, like the tragic boy king Tutankhamun, may be put to rest," he wrote.

Egyptologists are still asked about the curse. What did it say? Where was it located? One hundred years after the tomb's discovery, rumors still swirl. But here's the truth:

There were no curses inscribed *anywhere* in Tutankhamun's tomb. Not above the door, or on the sarcophagus, or on a magic brick beneath the chest of the pharaoh's internal organs. Not on a clay tablet, or at the base of a lamp. There wasn't a single curse. Not one. It was just a made-up story.

What is a curse other than a mean wish? And a mean wish doesn't have any power. It can't attack anyone, or plot revenge. It's just a harmless, mean wish.

A mean wish didn't eat Carter's canary. A hungry cobra did.

A mean wish didn't kill Lord Carnarvon. Blood poisoning did.

A mean wish didn't cause all the lights in Cairo to go out at the exact time of Carnarvon's death. A power cut—common in Cairo—did.

And a mean wish didn't cause the deaths, illnesses, or misfortunes of all those other people, either. Sure, listed together it *seems* like a curse had something to do with it. But think of all the people who visited the tomb in the years Carter excavated. Think of all the workers who dug and guarded and crated and carried. Think of those who were closest to the objects in the tomb. Harry Burton, who photographed every artifact, died in 1940, at age sixty. Alfred

Lucas, the chemist who left the king's mummy out in the blistering sun, died in 1950, at seventy-nine. Dr. Derry, who autopsied the mummy, died in 1969 at the advanced age of eighty-seven. And what about Howard Carter? If anyone should have been cursed, it was he. He found the tomb, opened it, and spent ten years removing everything from inside it. But a curse didn't kill him. Cancer did.

Science and logic have shown there is no such thing as the mummy's curse. It is nothing but a knot of rumor and superstition. Untangle that knot and what do we find? Just a myth—one that is often mistaken for fact. A myth—one that diminishes the real-life Tutankhamun. He wasn't a malevolent spirit. Rather, he was a boy who died too young.

Tutankhamun's body still lies in the tomb where it has rested for more than three thousand years. But it is no longer inside the pink-granite sarcophagus with its delicate carvings of goddesses. Now the sarcophagus stands open and empty. The king's outermost coffin has gone to the museum in Cairo. And his remains have been placed in a temperature-controlled glass case and tucked in a poorly lit corner against the far wall of the Antechamber. White linen covers him from neck to ankles. His exposed bare toes are withered and leathery. His uncovered face is black and cracked like dried earth.

Again and again, the tomb's *gaffir*, guardian, directs a beam of light onto the boy king's face so the tourists who crowd the space can see more clearly.

Some people gape, transfixed by the sight.

Others turn away, feeling suddenly uncomfortable.

And one person whispers words of thanks to the teenaged boy who has given so much—his tomb, his treasures, his mortal remains and eternal peace—in the name of science and knowledge.

A prayer—engraved on a wishing cup found in the tomb—is whispered, too: *May your spirit live, may you spend millions of years, you who love Thebes, sitting with your face to the north wind, your eyes beholding happiness.*

TUTANKHAMUN'S PLACE IN HISTORY

Egyptologists have traditionally divided the long span of ancient Egyptian history into "Kingdoms" and "Intermediate Periods." Each of these is further divided into "Dynasties." A dynasty is a series of rulers belonging to one family. The precise dates of kingdoms and intermediate periods, however, are hard to pin down. So, too, are the exact dates of dynasties and the pharaohs who ruled during them. The reason? New evidence is constantly found and old evidence is continually reconsidered. This has led to an ongoing scholarly debate. The outline below (from Dr. J. J. Shirley, Managing Editor of the *Journal of Egyptian History* and Director of the Theban Tomb 110 Epigraphy & Research Field School) gives an overview of ancient Egypt's history. I have listed the names of the Eighteenth Dynasty in full; Tutankhamun and his immediate family, as well as their *possible* relationship (Egyptologists are still debating this, too) to the boy king, are highlighted in italics.

Early Dynastic Period: before 3000–2649 BCE

Lower and Upper Egypt are united, perhaps by the pharaoh Narmer, and the centuries that follow see a consolidation of pharaonic rule.

Dynasties: 1–2

Old Kingdom: ca. 2649–2150 BCE

This is the period when pharaohs built the Giza and other nearby pyramids as their resting places.

Dynasties: 3–6

First Intermediate Period: ca. 2150–2030 BCE

Confusion and chronic drought bring a breakdown of centralized government.

Dynasties: 8–10

Dynasty: 11 (first half)

Middle Kingdom: ca. 2030–1640 BCE

Egypt is reunited under one king and ruled by a series of strong pharaohs. Lower Nubia is brought fully under Egyptian control.

Dynasty: 11 (second half)

Dynasties: 12–13

Second Intermediate Period: ca. 1640–1540 BCE

Hyksos, a people from Asia, rule in the Delta. The Kushite Empire rules all of Nubia into southernmost Egypt. The rulers of Upper Egypt battle to reunite the country. Ahmose expels the Hyksos at the end of this period, giving rise to the New Kingdom.

Dynasties: 14–17

New Kingdom: ca. 1550–1070 BCE

Three dynasties of pharaohs rule over Egypt, bringing five hundred years of continuous rule. Egypt is at the height of its influence as an international power. The Valley of the Kings becomes the royal burial ground starting with Thutmose I.

18th Dynasty:

Ahmose I (ca. 1550–1525 BCE)

Amenhotep I (ca. 1525–1504 BCE)

Thutmose I (ca. 1504–1492 BCE)

Thutmose II (ca. 1492–1479 BCE)

Thutmose III (ca. 1479–1425 BCE)

Queen Hatshepsut as regent (ca. 1479–1473 BCE)

Queen Hatshepsut as ruler (ca. 1473–1458 BCE)

Amenhotep II (ca. 1427–1400 BCE)

Thutmose IV (ca. 1400–1390 BCE)

Amenhotep III (ca. 1390–1352 BCE)

Believed to be Tutankhamun's grandfather

Amenhotep IV, also called Akhenaten (ca. 1353–1336 BCE)

Believed to be Tutankhamun's father

Queen Neferneferuaten (throne name of Nefertiti) (ca. 1338–1336 BCE)

Possibly Tutankhamun's mother or his sister

Smenkhkare (ca. 1336 BCE)

Possibly Tutankhamun's uncle or his half brother

Tutankhamun (ca. 1336–1327 BCE)

Ay (ca. 1327–1323 BCE)

Horemheb (ca. 1323–1295 BCE)

Dynasties: 19–20

Third Intermediate Period: ca. 1070–713 BCE

By the end of the New Kingdom, Egypt is weak and bankrupt. The country is partly split between northern and southern rule.

Dynasties: 21–24

Kushite Period: ca. 712–664 BCE

The Nubian Kingdom based at Kerma takes control of Lower (northern) Nubia, and then Egypt. They rule in traditional pharaonic style until Assyrians sack Thebes in 663, effectively ending Nubian rule over Egypt.

Dynasty: 25

Late Dynastic Period: ca. 688–332 BCE

The sack of Thebes allows for Egyptian rule to return. Persians twice invade and take control over Egypt. Their rule is ended with Macedonian general Alexander the Great's conquest of the country in 332 BCE. Traditionally, the flight of King Nectanebo II from Upper Egypt is considered the end of native Egyptian rule (at least until the twentieth century) and thus the end of Egyptian dynasties.

Dynasties: 26–30

Macedonian and Ptolemaic Egypt: ca. 332–30 BCE

Alexander the Great throws off the Persians and makes himself ruler. Upon his death, his general Ptolemy succeeds him. Ptolemy's descendants will lead the country until the death of Cleopatra VII and Ptolemy XV, and the advent of Roman rule over Egypt.

BIBLIOGRAPHY

The starting point for piecing together this story was Howard Carter's three volumes, *The Tomb of Tut-ankh-amen*. I also depended on the Griffith Institute in the Ashmolean Museum, Oxford, UK, where Carter's journals, diaries, notebooks, and unpublished autobiographical notes, as well as a set of Harry Burton's photographs, are housed. I owe a debt of gratitude to T. G. H. James for his detailed and thoughtful biography of Carter. Thanks, too, to Mark Beynon for his colorful history of the mummy's curse, and to Charlotte Booth for her practical one.

Of course, researching this book would have been impossible without a visit to Egypt. Landscapes speak, and houses (or in this case, tombs) hold memories. In Cairo, I spent hours on the hot, stuffy second floor of the Cairo museum among the treasures of Tutankhamun. Even in their neat display cases, they remain mind-bogglingly gorgeous and poignantly moving. In the Valley of the Kings, I visited Carter's house, where I sat at his desk, wore his straw fedora, and held the horse-tail fan with which he once flicked away flies as he wrote up his excavation notes. I traveled along the winding road, glistening with white marble chips, that led into the Valley, too. And finally—excitement of excitements—I descended into Tutankhamun's tomb. I gazed at the rose-colored sarcophagus and peeked into the Treasury and the Annex. And I came face-to-face with the boy king in his temperature-controlled glass case. During this entire trip, I was fortunate to have the company of Essam Hamed, an Egyptologist from the American University in Cairo with a working knowledge of hieroglyphs. Essam was eloquent about the future of discovery in his country. "Egypt," he said, "is never exhausted of antiquities." He believes further artifacts will be found beneath the protecting sands. Other tombs? Other treasures? Time, and science, will tell.

PRIMARY SOURCES
Books

Carnarvon, [Fifth] Earl of, and Howard Carter. *Five Years' Exploration at Thebes: A Record of Work Done 1907–1911.* London: Oxford University Press, 1912.

Carnarvon, [Sixth] Earl of. *No Regrets.* London: Weidenfeld & Nicolson, 1976.

Carter, Howard. *The Tomb of Tutankhamun.* London: The Folio Society, 2013.

Caton-Thompson, Gertrude. *Mixed Memoirs.* Baltimore: Paradigm Press, 1983.

Cheiro. *True Ghost Stories.* London: The London Publishing Company, 1928.

Edwards, Amelia B. *Pharaohs, Fellahs and Explorers.* New York: Harper & Brothers, 1900.

Petrie, W. M. Flinders. *Seventy Years in Archaeology.* London: Methuen, 1931.

Vandenberg, Philipp. *The Curse of the Pharaohs.* London: Hodder and Stoughton, 1975.

Weigall, Arthur. *The Glory of the Pharaohs.* New York: G.P. Putnam's Sons, 1923.

Weigall, Arthur. *Tutankhamen and Other Essays*. New York: George Doran, 1924.

Magazine and Newspaper Articles

"Carnarvon's Death Spreads Theory About Vengeance," *New York Times*, April 6, 1923.

"Carter Goes to Luxor to Reopen the Tomb," *New York Times*, October 4, 1923.

"George J. Gould Dies in Villa in France," *New York Times*, May 17, 1923.

"Only Five Entered the Tomb," *New York Times*, February 17, 1923.

"Under a Curse: Archaeologist's Death Suicide in a Taxi," *Times* (UK), September 10, 1924.

Carter, Howard, and P. White. "The Tomb of the Bird," *Pearson's Magazine*, November 1923.

Dean, Geoffrey. "The Curse of the Pharaohs," *World Medicine*, June 1975.

Robinson, Bertram Fletcher. "A Priestess of Death," *Daily Express* (UK), June 3, 1904.

Other Documents

Carter, Howard. Notebook Entry, October 23, 1926, Carter MSS, Griffith Institute.

Carter, Howard. Notes, Diary, and Articles Relating to the Theban Royal Necropolis and the Tomb of Tutankhamen, January 22, 1925, Carter MSS, Griffith Institute.

Carter, Howard. Unpublished Autobiography Draft and Notes, Griffith Institute.

Llewellyn, Francis, to John E. Newberry, February 2, 1891, Newberry Correspondence, Griffith Institute.

SECONDARY SOURCES
Books

Beynon, Mark. *London's Curse: Murder, Black Magic and Tutankhamun in the 1920s West End.* Stroud, UK: The History Press, 2011.

Booth, Charlotte. *The Curse of the Mummy and Other Mysteries of Ancient Egypt.* Oxford, UK: Oneworld Publications, 2009.

Breasted, Charles. *Pioneer to the Past: The Story of James Henry Breasted.* New York: Charles Scribner's Sons, 1948.

Breasted, James Henry. *Development of Religion and Thought in Ancient Egypt*. New York: Charles Scribner's Sons, 1912.

Carnarvon, Countess of. *Lady Almina and the Real Downton Abbey: The Lost Legacy of Highclere Castle*. London: Hodder & Stoughton, 2011.

Cook, Steven A. *The Struggle for Egypt: From Nasser to Tahrir Square*. New York: Oxford University Press, 2012.

Emberling, George, ed. *Pioneers to the Past: American Archaeologists in the Middle East, 1919–1920*. Chicago: Oriental Institute Museum Publications, 2010.

Fagan, Brian. *Lord and Pharaoh*. London: Routledge, Taylor & Francis Group, 2015.

Frayling, Christopher. *The Face of Tutankhamun*. London: Faber & Faber, 1992.

Harrison, Paul. *The Curse of the Pharaohs' Tombs: Tales of the Unexpected Since the Days of Tutankhamun*. Barnsley, UK: Pen and Sword Archaeology, 2017.

Hoving, Thomas. *Tutankhamun: The Untold Story*. New York: Simon and Schuster, 1978.

James, T. G. H. *Howard Carter: The Path to Tutankhamun*. London: Tauris Parke Paperbacks, 2000.

Lace, William W. *The Curse of King Tut*. Mankato, MN: Capstone, 2008.

Lockhart, J. G. *Curses, Lucks and Talismans*. London: Geoffrey Bles, 1938.

Mansfield, Peter. *The British in Egypt*. New York: Holt, Rinehart and Winston, 1972.

Pollard, Lisa. *Nurturing the Nation: The Family Politics of Modernizing, Colonizing, and Liberating Egypt 1805–1923*. Berkeley: University of California Press, 2005.

Reeves, Nicholas. *Into the Mummy's Tomb: The Real-Life Discovery of Tutankhamun's Treasures*. New York: Scholastic/Madison Press, 1992.

Reeves, Nicholas, and John H. Taylor. *Howard Carter: Before Tutankhamun*. New York: Harry N. Abrams, Inc., 1993.

Romer, John. *Valley of the Kings*. New York: Morrow, 1981.

Taylor, John H. *Egyptian Mummies*. London: British Museum Press, 2010.

Tyldesley, Joyce. *Tutankhamun: The Search for an Egyptian King*. New York: Basic Books, 2012.

Wilson, Jeremy. *Lawrence of Arabia: The Authorized Biography of T. E. Lawrence.* New York: Atheneum, 1990.

Magazines and Journal Articles

"The Facts Behind the Curse of Tutankhamun: Fake News from Beyond the Grave," https://www .historyanswers.co.uk/ancient/the-curse-of -tutankhamun-and-fake-news-from-beyond-the-grave/.

Bennett, J. "The Restoration Inscription of Tut'ankhamun," *Journal of Egyptian Archaeology*, 25, 1939.

Handwerk, Brian. "Curse of the Mummy," https:// www.nationalgeographic.com/history/archaeology /curse-of-the-mummy/.

Nelson, Mark R. "The Mummy's Curse: Historical Cohort Study," *BMJ*, December 21–28, 2002.

Soussi, Alasdair. "Why Howard Carter's Discovery of King Tut's Tomb Will Never Be Forgotten," https://www.thenational.ae/arts-culture /why-howard-carter-s-discovery-of-king-tut-s-tomb -will-never-be-forgotten-1.842543.

SOURCE NOTES

It was said . . .

"Death will slay with . . .": Charlotte Booth, *The Curse of the Mummy and Other Mysteries of Ancient Egypt*, Oxford, UK: Oneworld Publications, 2009, 186.

"O anyone who enters . . .": Mark Beynon, *London's Curse: Murder, Black Magic and Tutankhamun in the 1920s West End*, Stroud, UK: The History Press, 2011, 32.

"It is I who . . .": Booth, 187.

Chapter 1: Sands of the Past

"Now when his majesty . . .": J. Bennett, "The Restoration Inscription of Tut'ankhamun," *Journal of Egyptian Archaeology, 25*, 1939, 8.

"The [Egyptians] all rejoice and celebrate. . .": Brian Fagan, *Lord and Pharaoh*, London: Routledge, Taylor & Francis Group, 2015, 87.

"seat of the mind . . .": James Henry Breasted, *Development of Religion and Thought in Ancient Egypt*, New York: Charles Scribner's Sons, 1912, 44.

"At every step . . .": Amelia B. Edwards, *Pharaohs, Fellahs and Explorers*, New York: Harper & Brothers, 1900, 13–14.

"The exploration is a kind of chase . . .": ibid., 12.

Chapter 2: The "City of the Dead"

"'The records of the past' . . .": Arthur Weigall, *The Glory of the Pharaohs*, New York: G.P. Putnam's Sons, 1923, 101.

"'My first important find' . . .": Fagan, 79.

"'I wonder what I will find next' . . .": ibid.

It was said . . .

"'A gray cat!' . . .": Arthur Weigall, *Tutankhamen and Other Essays*, New York: George Doran, 1924, 140.

"'Keep the cat away' . . .": ibid.

Chapter 3: Enter Howard Carter

"'He is a friend of mine' . . .": Nicholas Reeves, *Into the Mummy's Tomb: The Real-Life Discovery of Tutankhamun's Treasures*, New York: Scholastic/Madison Press, 1992, 14.

"'A stubborn man is' . . .": ibid.

"I have nothing to say . . .": Howard Carter, autobiographical notes intended for book, Carter MSS., vi.2.1-14, Griffith Institute, Oxford, UK.

"drawing . . . portraits of pet parrots . . .": ibid.

"hooked . . .": ibid.

"a non-gentleman artist . . .": Francis Llewellyn to John E. Newberry, February 2, 1891, Griffith Institute, Oxford, UK, Newberry Correspondence, 1.2/9.

"on the eve of an adventure . . .": Howard Carter, autobiographical notes intended for book, Carter MSS., vi.2.1-14, Griffith Institute, Oxford, UK.

"unconsidered trifles . . .": W. M. Flinders Petrie, *Seventy Years in Archaeology*, London: Methuen, 1931, 19.

"the observation of small things . . .": ibid.

"played" and "perplexed": Nicholas Reeves and John H. Taylor, *Howard Carter: Before Tutankhamun*, New York: Harry N. Abrams, Inc., 1993, 40.

"The indignity of letting . . .": Petrie, 192.

"The Egyptians must do . . .": Lisa Pollard, *Nurturing the Nation: The Family Politics of Modernizing, Colonizing, and Liberating Egypt: 1805–1923*, Berkeley: University of California Press, 2005, 98.

"'Egypt for the Egyptians!' . . .": Steven A. Cook, *The Struggle for Egypt: From Nasser to Tahrir Square*, New York: Oxford University Press, 2012, 47.

"dirty" and "dishonest": Jeremy Wilson, *Lawrence of Arabia: The Authorized Biography of T. E. Lawrence*, New York: Atheneum, 1990, 100.

"It is ridiculous . . .": Peter Mansfield, *The British in Egypt*, New York: Holt, Rinehart and Winston, 1972, 314.

It was said . . .

"As I looked into . . .": Cheiro, *True Ghost Stories*, London: The London Publishing Company, 1928, 52.

"'It radiates evil!' . . .": Bertram Fletcher Robinson, "A Priestess of Death," *Daily Express* (UK), June 3, 1904, 1.

"The priestess had only . . .": ibid.

"to do her worst . . .": J. G. Lockhart, *Curses, Lucks and Talismans*, London: Geoffrey Bles, 1938, 179.

Chapter 4: Ten Seasons Beneath the Theban Sun

"'I think we should' . . .": Fagan, 98.

"'No, we select one area' . . .": ibid.

"'I'll pitch my tent' . . .": ibid.

"tommyrot": T. G. H. James, *Howard Carter: The Path to Tutankhamun*, London: Tauris Parke Paperbacks, 2000, 213.

"spoke to [the earl] as if . . .": ibid., 283.

"I shall never forget . . .": [Fifth] Earl of Carnarvon and Howard Carter, *Five Years' Exploration at Thebes: A Record of Work Done 1907–1911*, London: Oxford University Press, 1912, Carnarvon's Introduction.

"If I had not been an archaeologist . . .": John Romer, *Valley of the Kings*, New York: Morrow, 1981, 201.

"The Valley of the Kings is now exhausted . . .": ibid., 293.

"sometimes depressed and sometimes happy . . .": James, 216.

"nearly dotty": ibid.

It was said . . .

"It is Coptic": [Sixth] Earl of Carnarvon, *No Regrets*, London: Weidenfeld & Nicolson, 1976, 129.

Chapter 5: A Bird of Gold That Will Bring Good Luck

"It shall belong to [you]": Charles Breasted, *Pioneer to the Past: The Story of James Henry Breasted*, New York: Charles Scribner's Sons, 1948, 329.

"'It's a bird of gold' . . .": James, 251.

"digging with sticks . . .": Thomas Hoving, *Tutankhamun: The Untold Story*, New York: Simon and Schuster, 1978, 77.

"'It is the tomb' . . .": ibid., 79.

"Anything, literally anything . . .": Howard Carter, *The Tomb of Tutankhamun*, London: The Folio Society, 2013, 43.

"AT LAST HAVE MADE WONDERFUL DISCOVERY. . .": James, 252.

"'Let's go down' . . .": Fagan, 119.

"'Plunderers [have] entered it' . . .": Carter, *Tomb*, 45.

"Darkness and black space . . .": ibid.

"Strange animals, statues and gold . . .": ibid.

"'Can you see anything?'": ibid.

"Yes, wonderful things . . .": ibid.

It was said . . .

"'An evil eye has been cast' . . .": Howard Carter and P. White, "The Tomb of the Bird," *Pearson's Magazine*, November 1923, 433.

Chapter 6: Under Cover of Darkness

"It is the most beautiful thing . . .": Hoving, 98.

"This is going to take years.": Fagan, 128.

"pestered morning, noon and night . . .": The Countess of Carnarvon, *Lady Almina and the Real Downton Abbey: The Lost Legacy of Highclere Castle*, London: Hodder & Stoughton, 2011, 150.

It was said . . .

"Rightly or wrongly, I sent this warning . . .": Cheiro, 15.

Chapter 7: Early Days in the Tomb

"It is an unheard of thing . . .": Hoving, 163.

"We are going to have a concert . . .": "Only Five Entered the Tomb," *New York Times*,

February 17, 1923, 1.

"'I see a wall of' . . .": Hoving, 195.

"It is I who hinder the sand . . .": Joyce Tyldesley, *Tutankhamun: The Search for an Egyptian King*, New York: Basic Books, 2012, loc. 3413.

"fill the Valley with a resounding blast . . .": Carter, *Tomb*, 140.

"For the first time in all my experience . . .": Hoving, 196.

"This afternoon I had standing around me . . .": James, 283.

"with a noise like a champagne cork.": Tyldesley, loc. 1308.

"No power on earth could . . .": Christopher Frayling, *The Face of Tutankhamun*, London: Faber & Faber, 1992, 28.

"ransacked" and "rifled": George Emberling, ed., *Pioneers to the Past: American Archaeologists in the Middle East 1919–1920*, Chicago: Oriental Institute Museum Publications, 2010, 89.

"I have been feeling very unhappy today . . .": James, 293.

"It takes us all we know to restrain Carnarvon . . .": ibid., 238.

"mooning around" and "arranging the pendants": ibid.

"rather poorly.": Countess of Carnarvon, 154.

"The old man is very seedy . . .": ibid.

It was said . . .
"I see the hand of the pharaoh . . .": Frayling, 43.

"the most dire punishment.": ibid.

"That is why I ask . . .": ibid.

Chapter 8: And at the Continental-Savoy Hotel . . .
"I have heard the call . . .": Frayling, 38.

"'A bird is scratching at my face' . . .": Booth, 185.

"'Pharaoh, I am returning to you' . . .": Beynon, 34.

Chapter 9: Curses!
"curse crazy.": Booth, 184.

"The Earl could have . . .": Frayling, 42.

"Death will slay with its wings . . .": Booth, 186.

"It is I who hinder the sand . . .": ibid.

"And I will kill all those . . .": Frayling, 50.

"It is I who drive back . . .": Booth, 187.

"It is too much to believe that some [ghost] . . .": "Carter Goes to Luxor to Reopen the Tomb," *New York Times*, October 4, 1923, 1.

"'Bunkum!'": "Carnarvon's Death Spreads Theories About Vengeance," *New York Times*, April 6, 1923, 1.

"there would not be any archaeologists . . .": ibid.

"rather tired and washed out . . .": James, 299.

It was said . . .

"Considerable mystery surrounds the nature . . .": "George J. Gould Dies in Villa in France," *New York Times*, May 17, 1923, 1.

"spirits of the pharaohs . . .": Paul Harrison, *The Curse of the Pharaohs' Tombs: Tales of the Unexpected Since the Days of Tutankhamun*, Barnsley, UK: Pen and Sword Archaeology, 2017, 27.

"drew the last breath out of him.": ibid.

"I knew there was a curse on me.": "Under a Curse: Archaeologist's Death Suicide in a Taxi," *Times* (UK), September 10, 1924, 1.

"I have succumbed to a curse . . .": William W. Lace, *The Curse of King Tut*, Mankato, MN: Capstone, 2008, 66.

Chapter 10: Shrines, Sarcophagus, and Coffins

"The government no longer discusses . . .": Tyldesley, loc. 1387.

"We had to squeeze in and out . . .": Carter, *Tomb*, 147.

"'I have seen yesterday' . . .": Hoving, 264.

"Past and present . . .": Carter, *Tomb*, 153.

"a gasp of wonderment escaped . . .": ibid., 155.

"Oh, Mother Nut!": ibid., 156.

"The ministry [under the direction of Morcos Bey Hanna] . . .": Hoving, 287.

"Owing to impossible restrictions": James, 337.

Chapter 11: The Mummy Unwrapped

"It is ruined!": Howard Carter, Carter Diary, January 22, 1925, Notes, Diary, and Articles Relating to the Theban Royal Necropolis and the Tomb of Tutankhamen, Carter MSS., TAA.1.2.1, Griffith Institute, Oxford, UK.

"at an almost painful tension . . .": Carter, *Tomb*, 172.

"How great must have been the wealth": ibid., 177.

"head of mystery" and "seeing with the head of a god": John H. Taylor, *Egyptian Mummies*, London: British Museum Press, 2010, 47.

"refined and cultured . . .": Carter, *Tomb*, 199.

Chapter 12: Fabulous Finds

"The King's mummy . . .": Howard Carter, Notebook Entry, October 23, 1926, Carter MSS., TAA 1.2.1., Griffith Institute, Oxford, UK.

"topsy-turvy": Carter, *Tomb*, 274.

"The shadows move . . .": ibid., 133.

It was said . . .

"the old and original Egyptian . . .": James, 414.

Chapter 13: Work Complete

"a long and steady plod.": James, 414.

"I pitied [Carter] cooped up . . .": Gertrude Caton-Thompson, *Mixed Memoirs*, Baltimore: Paradigm Press, 1983, 148.

"We can only say how lucky . . .": James, 438.

"There is a great danger in haste . . .": Carter, *Tomb*, 121.

It was said . . .

"the curse of the pharaohs": "The Facts Behind the Curse of Tutankhamun: Fake News from Beyond the Grave," https://www.historyanswers.co.uk/ancient /the-curse-of-tutankhamun-and-fake-news-from-beyond-the-grave/.

"Death shall come on swift wings . . .": ibid.

"I really cannot stand any more horrors.": ibid.

Chapter 14: Exit Carter

"In many ways the discovery . . .": Alasdair Soussi, "Why Howard Carter's Discovery of King Tut's Tomb Will Never Be Forgotten," https://www.thenational .ae/arts-culture/why-howard-carter-s-discovery-of-king-tut-s-tomb-will -never-be-forgotten-1.842543.

Howard Carter gravestone epitaph: Tyldesley, loc. 1578.

It was said . . .

"Look, I'm kicking the most expensive thing . . .": Booth, 190.

Chapter 15: Space Travelers, Poison, and Murderous Mold

"At that moment of discovery . . .": Booth, 190.

"old people who were present . . .": Geoffrey Dean, "The Curse of the Pharaohs," *World Medicine*, June 1975, 17.

"The idea that an underground tomb . . .": Brian Handwerk, "Curse of the Mummy," https://www.nationalgeographic.com/history/archaeology /curse-of-the-mummy/.

"Perhaps finally it . . .": Mark R. Nelson, "The Mummy's Curse: Historical Cohort Study," *BMJ*, December 21–28, 2002, 1484.

"May your spirit live . . .": Tyldesley, loc. 1578.

PHOTOGRAPH AND ILLUSTRATION CREDITS

INDEX

Page numbers in *italics* refer to illustrations.

ABOUT THE AUTHOR

Candace Fleming writes picture books and middle grade and young adult works of narrative nonfiction and biographies. Among her nonfiction titles are Sibert Award–winner *Honeybee: The Busy Life of Apis Mellifera*; *Giant Squid*; *Amelia Lost: The Life and Disappearance of Amelia Earhart*; *The Family Romanov: Murder, Rebellion & the Fall of Imperial Russia*; and *The Rise and Fall of Charles Lindbergh*, winner of the YALSA Excellence in Nonfiction for Young Adults Award. She is the recipient of the *Los Angeles Times* Book Prize, and the Orbis Pictus Award, as well as the two-time recipient of the *Boston Globe/Horn Book* Award for Nonfiction, a YALSA's Excellence in Nonfiction finalist, the ALA Sibert Honor, and SCBWI's Golden Kite Award.